TRANSFORMATION

CAC Publishing
Center for Action and Contemplation
cac.org

"*Oneing*" is an old English word that was used by Lady Julian of Norwich (1342–1416) to describe the encounter between God and the soul. The Center for Action and Contemplation proudly borrows the word to express the divine unity that stands behind all of the divisions, dichotomies, and dualisms in the world. We pray and publish with Jesus' words, "that all may be one" (John 17:21).

EDITOR:
Vanessa Guerin

ASSOCIATE EDITOR:
Shirin McArthur

PUBLISHER:
The Center for Action and Contemplation

ADVISORY BOARD:
David Benner
James Danaher
Ilia Delio, OSF
Sheryl Fullerton
Stephen Gaertner, OPraem
Ruth Patterson

Design and Composition by Nelson Kane Design

Cover and title pages: Top view of Hopi "butterfly vase." The six insects are actually moths, which represent the four directions plus the zenith and nadir. From Smithsonian Institution, Bureau of American Ethnology.

Oneing

VOLUME 5 NO. 1

Transformation implies journey, pilgrimage, a crossing over. It is not something we can will upon ourselves or decide that it should happen to us. Rather, it is something that happens to us as a result, for example, of some experience on the journey or of some encounter. It is gift.

—Ruth Patterson

A s I WAS READING through the very fine articles in this edition of *Oneing*, I was struck by the fact that each fell into one of three categories: (1) authors who take a scholarly, theological look at the word *transformation*—the theme of this edition; (2) those who describe one or more authentic, transformative experiences; and (3) those who incorporate both the intellectual (head) and the experiential (heart) elements of transformation.

In her article, "Wild Things Tamed," Ruth Patterson illustrates how it is when we move from "a particular way of thinking and being and soar into a new world of awareness...across the threshold from a two-dimensional world where everything is cut and dried into a three-dimensional one that is inhabited by wonder, mystery, and an unknowing that is, paradoxically, profoundly recognizable at a level beyond the head."

A particularly intuitive description of this transition "beyond the head" is told by Tiffany Keesey in her article, "Repairing My Inner Two States." Keesey became "increasingly aware of the unresolved paradoxes within" herself on a recent journey to Israel, and this "holy land" experience helped her to reconcile and embrace the relationship between her teenage, passionately Christian, fundamental self and her more mature, thirty-something self. Keesey masterfully tells her transformative story by cleverly referring to her inner selves in the third person.

With the passion of youth comes an impatience which Sam Shriver honestly discusses in "Divine Patience." Drawing upon the wisdom of Rainer Maria Rilke, Shriver discovers that his path toward transformation includes the "need to develop a capacity to endure the feelings that cause me uncertainty, insecurity, and fear—feelings that make me impatient. The ability to be patient with myself, in other words, is the ability to *be* myself." Taking to "the road" for three months, like so many pilgrims before him, he gets lost, struggles with solitude, and comes home "overwhelmingly comfortable in [his] own skin."

In sharing one of her own transformative experiences, scholar and theologian Cynthia Bourgeault gives the reader an insight that can only come from years of experiencing great suffering and great love (the keys to transformation, as Richard Rohr teaches). In "The Bell Rack of My Selfhood," Bourgeault writes:

> As a good student of Centering Prayer, I had been patiently working to dismantle my false self, assuming that my "true self" would be what was left when the illusory pretender was exposed. But, as the raw intimacy of the work with Rafe [her "beloved jousting partner"] intensified, we both began to notice that it was not the best side of ourselves that God seemed to be calling forth in the crucible of transformation, but, strangely, the *worst*—maybe because that's where the seeds of our redeemed essence were, in fact, planted.

Christopher Spatz, in his article, "The Exhilarations of Lymphoma: A Year in the Life," discovers his "crucible of transformation" in a rather unique way after undergoing months of chemotherapy and radiation for an aggressive form of cancer. During the treatment, he came to a place where, as he tells it, "I felt a peace that allowed me to really live in the present moment…and to forgive the many inconveniences in my life and livelihood—most of which seemed insignificant now." But, to his dismay, "the end of treatment created a void and [his] erstwhile resentments and irritations came streaming back in." Rather than wallow in these old familiar patterns, however, his awakening occurred when he realized that his time in treatment "offered a tangible model of what still could be."

These and many more powerful examples of transformative experiences in this edition of *Oneing* are beautifully balanced with the scholarly undergirding of authors like David Benner, James Danaher, Richard Rohr, Brittian Bullock, Mike Morrell, and others who help us better understand the gift of transformation.

Vanessa Guerin,
Editor

CONTRIBUTORS

RICHARD ROHR is a Franciscan priest of the New Mexico Province and the Founding Director of the Center for Action and Contemplation (CAC) in Albuquerque, New Mexico. An internationally recognized author and spiritual leader, Fr. Richard teaches primarily on incarnational mysticism, non-dual consciousness, and contemplation, with a particular emphasis on how these affect the social justice issues of our time. Along with many recorded conferences, he is the author of numerous books, including the newly published *The Divine Dance: The Trinity and Your Transformation* (with Mike Morrell) and *A Spring Within Us: A Book of Daily Meditations*. To learn more about Fr. Richard Rohr and the CAC, visit https://cac.org/richard-rohr/richard-rohr-ofm/.

JAMES P. DANAHER, PhD, is Professor of Philosophy at Nyack College, Nyack, New York, and the author of numerous books, including *Philosophical Imagination, Jesus' Copernican Revolution, The Second Truth, Contemplative Prayer*, and *Jesus after Modernity*. He has published over seventy articles that have appeared in a variety of philosophy and theology journals. To learn more about James Danaher, visit http://www.jamespdanaher.com/.

DAVID G. BENNER is an internationally known depth psychologist and author whose passion and calling has been the understanding and facilitation of awakening and transformation. His educational background includes an Honors BA in psychology from McMaster University, an MA and PhD in clinical psychology from York University, and post-doctoral studies at the Chicago Institute of Psychoanalysis. He has authored or edited thirty books that have been translated into nineteen foreign languages, including *Soulful Spirituality, Spirituality and the Awakening Self, Presence and Encounter*, and *Human Being and Becoming*. To learn more about David Benner, visit http://www.drdavidgbenner.ca/.

THE REV. DR. CYNTHIA BOURGEAULT is a modern-day mystic, Episcopal priest, writer, and internationally recognized retreat leader. Cynthia divides her time between solitude at her seaside hermitage in Maine and traveling globally to teach the Christian contemplative and Wisdom path. A long-time advocate of Centering Prayer, Cynthia has worked closely with Thomas

Keating and Bruno Barnhart. She is the founding Director of both The Contemplative Society and the Aspen Wisdom School and a member of the Living School for Action and Contemplation's core faculty. Cynthia is the author of numerous books, including *The Heart of Centering Prayer* and *The Holy Trinity and the Law of Three*. To learn more about her Four Voices method of spiritual discernment, based on listening appreciatively to each voice in the inner bell rack, visit http://www.contemplative.org/events/cynthia-bourgeaults-four-voices-method-of-discernment/.

Sam Mowe is editor in chief at the Garrison Institute, a nonprofit organization dedicated to exploring the intersection of wisdom, science, and engaged action in the world. He is a frequent contributor to *The Sun*, *Spirituality & Health*, and *Tricycle: The Buddhist Review*. To learn more about the Garrison Institute, visit https://www.garrisoninstitute.org/.

Mary Evelyn Tucker, PhD, is co-director of the Forum on Religion and Ecology at Yale University, where she teaches in an MA program between the School of Forestry & Environmental Studies and the Divinity School. With John Grim, she organized ten conferences on World Religions and Ecology at Harvard and co-authored *Ecology and Religion*. With Brian Swimme, she wrote *Journey of the Universe*, and she is the executive director of the Emmy Award-winning film, *Journey*. Mary Evelyn served on the International Earth Charter Drafting Committee and was a member of the Earth Charter International Council. To learn more about Mary Evelyn Tucker, visit https://environment.yale.edu/profile/tucker.

Julianne Warren holds a PhD in wildlife ecology and conservation biology. She taught at New York University, where she won a 2013 Martin Luther King, Jr., Faculty Award for her work with students in the climate justice movement. She is author of *Aldo Leopold's Odyssey*, an intellectual biography tracing the historical development of Leopold's land health concept. Presently, Julianne is working on an interdisciplinary environmental studies text and her other work-in-progress is a triptych of volumes exploring Earth's generativity. To learn more about Julianne Warren, visit https://www.coyotetrail.net/biography.

Sam Shriver is a writer, activist, and part-time tour guide in China. He is working to galvanize support for the growing men's movement, both to give men space to discuss healthy manhood and to hold men accountable for gender equality. Sam graduated from Boston College in 2014 with a major in history and a minor in Mandarin Chinese. He has a passion for east-west relations, focusing on the relationship between the USA and China. As a tour assistant with Sino Immersions, Sam loves to share his knowledge of Chinese language, history, and culture.

Wm Paul Young is author of the best-selling novel, *The Shack*. In this innovative, yet true-to-Scripture exploration of Trinity, Paul wrestles with the timeless question, "Where is God in a world of suffering and pain?" Paul has "the imagination of a writer and the passion of a theologian," as Eugene Peterson says. His recent work of fiction, *Eve*, offers breathtaking discoveries that challenge traditional beliefs about who we are and how we're made, helping us see each other as our Creator does—complete, unique, and not constrained by cultural rules or limitations. To learn more about Wm Paul Young, visit http://wmpaulyoung.com/wm-paul-young-about/.

Timothy King is a graduate of North Park University with degrees in both theology and philosophy. He worked as a community organizer for the Industrial Areas Foundation on the South Side of Chicago and served for seven years at Sojourners in Washington, DC. Tim has been a guest on many radio shows and podcasts and has been interviewed for various print and online publications, including *ABC News, the BBC, CNN, TIME, Christianity Today, The Christian Post*, and *The Daily Beast*. He currently lives and works at his family's farm in New Hampshire and enjoys thinking and writing about farming, food, and faith. To learn more about Timothy King, visit http://timothymichaelking.com/ or follow him on Twitter @tmking.

Christopher Spatz, the Center for Action and Contemplation's Resource Center Manager, administers all components of CAC's online bookstore and visitor center. In addition, Chris serves as the Center's facilities manager. Inspired by the glorious desert of New Mexico, Chris relocated to Albuquerque, New Mexico, from his hometown, Las Vegas, Nevada, in 1993. He holds a Bachelor of Fine Arts degree in Studio Art, with an emphasis in photography, from the University of New Mexico. Chris' family is comprised of his partner, Larry Davis, three Great Danes, two slithery snakes, and one yellow-bellied turtle. Christopher Spatz may be contacted at cspatznm@gmail.com.

Tiffany Keesey is a social activist and a student in the Living School for Action and Contemplation. After graduating as a Regents Scholar from UCLA, she became one of the founding members of Invisible Children. She then founded a consulting practice in which she partners with nonprofits and social enterprises to build values-driven organizations and teams. In the Living School, Tiffany is studying how leaders can develop a personal spiritual practice that deeply sustains their work in the world. In 2016,

Tiffany co-founded a company called WIDEN, which hosts gatherings for millennials to pursue spiritual depth and transformation in a collective commitment to renew the world. She is currently pursuing her yoga certification. To learn more about Tiffany Keesey, visit https://www. linkedin.com/in/tiffanykeesey.

Paula D'Arcy, a former psychotherapist, leads retreats and seminars worldwide and is a frequent teacher in the sabbatical program at Oblate School of Theology in San Antonio, Texas. The work of Red Bird Foundation, Paula's non-profit organization, includes prison retreats and talks and the gathering of small groups of individuals—including Israeli and Palestinian men and women—to foster widening awareness of the world's ongoing work toward freedom and peace. She is the author of numerous books, including *Gift of the Red Bird* and *Waking Up to This Day*, and the newly released *Stars at Night* and *The Divine Spark*. Paula makes her home in Texas. To learn more about Paula D'Arcy and her foundation, visit http://www. redbirdfoundation.com/.

The Rev. Dr. Ruth Patterson, a Presbyterian minister, was the first woman to be ordained as a minister in Ireland. Ruth is Director of Restoration Ministries, a non-denominational Christian organization committed to peace and reconciliation based in Northern Ireland. In addition, she produces annual scripture guidelines for Faith and Friendship, an organization in Northern Ireland inspired by Jean Vanier, the founder of *L'Arche*—an international movement for people with learning difficulties. Ruth has authored several books, including *A Farther Shore*, *Journeying Towards Reconciliation*, *Proclaiming the Promise*, *Looking Back to Tomorrow*, and *The Gaze of Love*. To learn more about Ruth Patterson, visit http://www. restorationministries.co.uk/index.php/about-us/ruth-patterson.

Mark Longhurst is a United Church of Christ pastor, writer, and blogger. A longtime social-justice activist, a dedicated yoga practitioner, and the father of two young boys, his discovery of Christianity's mystical tradition through Fr. Richard Rohr and the Living School for Action and Contemplation has renewed his faith and become a passionate life pursuit. He pastors the First Congregational Church in Williamstown, Massachusetts, and enjoys leading social-justice-oriented Christians into engagement with the arts and deeper experience of contemplative practices. Mark is the editor of the website Ordinary Mystic, where he blogs regularly and curates reflections from others seeking to follow a mystical path in their everyday lives. To learn more about Mark Longhurst, visit http://www. ordinarymystic.net/.

BRITTIAN BULLOCK, MA, MHP, is a clinical therapist utilizing contemplative-based counseling to work with a wide range of clients, from the chronically suicidal to those searching for spiritual direction. He also teaches graduate courses that focus on theories of human development, ecology, and the impact of civilization on mental health. Brittian lived for over a decade in a neo-monastic community, drawing on the rich tradition of both Catholic and Protestant mystics. He is a writer, speaker, and teacher interested in primal spirituality and heartful living. Brittian, his wife, and their four children live near Portland, Oregon. To learn more about Brittian Bullock's ongoing meditations on trauma, wholeness, therapy, and a life well-lived, visit http://BrittianBullock.com/.

MIKE MORRELL is Communications Director for the Integral Theology think tank Presence International. He is co-founder of The Buzz Seminar and a founding organizer of the Wild Goose Festival. Mike curates contemplative and community experiences via Relational Yoga, the ManKind Project, (H) Opp, and Authentic North Carolina, taking joy in holding space for the extraordinary transformation that can take place at the intersection of anticipation, imagination, and radical acceptance. Mike is also an avid writer, publishing consultant, author coach, futurist, and curator of the book-reviewing community at TheSpeakeasy.info. He lives with his wife and two daughters in North Carolina. To learn more about Mike Morrell's ongoing exploration of spirit, culture, and permaculture, visit http://MikeMorrell. org/.

INTRODUCTION

THE WORD "TRANSFORMATION" has become more common in recent decades, especially in spiritual circles, often replacing the previously more common word "conversion." This has happened for many reasons and reveals a significant evolution in understanding. Etymologically, of course, conversion means a turn or turnabout. It was largely used to describe a change in religious affiliation or having undergone some kind of emotional or intellectual experience—often religious in nature. Eventually, this experience became so superficial that the word began to be used in a humorous or derogatory way.

Perhaps many of us stopped using the word conversion—except in bona fide insider conversations—because it was so often found not to be a true *turning* so much as a turning inside the same space: a mere change of vocabulary or external group identification. It is almost as if we began to see a need to describe something else that was much more necessary and important: an actual, discernible change in one's inner state—and for the better!

Etymologically, transformation means a change in form, a move across, and even what is now called a "shape-shifter" in the world of story. It implies actual development, evolution, and change of consciousness, image, and form. The word is used to imply looking out from a genuinely new source and center, which usually means seeing things in a larger and more holistic way. A transformed person is a participatory self, an inclusive self, a generous self, revealing a measurable move toward compassion—and beyond protecting one's personal autonomy and small, egoic reference point. This change sometimes, but not necessarily, uses specifically religious language. Such language too often gets in the way of what is really happening—or not happening. The important difference is *one's observable capacity to include, forbear, appreciate, and understand.* Without these, there could not be any discussion of true transformation.

Richard Rohr

Transformation

By James P. Danaher

F OR MANY CHRISTIANS, their notion of truth is not transforming because their inherited concept of truth comes from Aristotle and the tradition that followed him. Aristotle had said that
human beings are involved in three basic activities: making, doing, and
knowing. When we make, we want to make what is beautiful; when
we do, we want to do what is good; and when we know, we want to
know what is true. Consequently, Western thinking since the time
of Aristotle has imagined truth as simply something to know. In the
modern era, our idea of truth became even more narrowly defined as
something to know after the model of mathematics; that is, as a kind
of knowing that is certain, objective, and precise.

I have argued elsewhere[1] that, if that is our idea of truth, we
will never understand the Gospels, since the truth of the Gospels is
nothing like the notion of truth we inherit from Aristotle and our early
modern ancestors. To begin with, Jesus' concept of truth is not a set
of doctrines to know and believe but a way to *be*. In fact, originally,
before the term "Christian" came into use, followers of Jesus identified

themselves as people of *The Way*. Jesus had said, "I am the way, and the truth, and the life" (see John 14:6). It was a truth that transformed his followers into a new way of life because it was rooted in a beauty and goodness so divine that it allowed those who embraced it to treat others as they wished others to treat them.[2] It was a truth so divinely beautiful and good that those who embraced it aspired to love even their enemies and give to others without expecting anything in return (see Luke 6:35). It was a truth so divinely beautiful and good that those who fell in love with it were able to rejoice in being poor in spirit, mournful, and meek. It was a truth which made people hunger and thirst for righteousness, rather than believing that they were righteous because of what they believed (see Matthew 5:3–6).

It seems clear from Jesus' teachings that what he sought to teach his followers was how *to be* as he was. Seventeen times throughout the Gospels, Jesus says, "follow me." What else could he mean but "*be* as I am"? The truth that Jesus taught was a way to be rather than something to know and believe. It seems strange that Christians put their faith in theologies and formulas for salvation when Jesus himself never mentions such things and gives us very little from which to form such epistemic truths. In fact, Jesus even refuses to answer questions from which we might form theologies and doctrines. Of the 183 questions asked of Jesus throughout the four Gospels, he answers only three. His usual response is to ask a question in return, answer a different question than the one asked, or simply refuse to answer. Furthermore, the three that he does answer have little to do with the objective nature of God or the world, but rather are about how we should respond to God and the world. The questions—"Teach us to pray" (see Luke 11:1), "How many times must we forgive?" (see Matthew 18:21), and "What is the greatest commandment?" (see Matthew 22:36)—are questions about us, and how we ought to be. Jesus answers them because he is trying to teach his followers a divine way of being in the world.

Interestingly, although Jesus answers only three of the many questions asked of him, he asks 307 questions throughout the Gospels. How do we make theology out of that? A seminary student once asked one of her professors why they never talk about Jesus in seminary, but only Paul. The professor responded, "You can't make theology out of Jesus." Indeed, instead of giving us a theology, or even enough from which to create a theology, Jesus offers his followers a way to *be*, as he

The truth that Jesus taught was a way to *be* rather than something to know and believe.

was, toward God and the world. Of course, the last thing we want to do is to love our enemies and live a life of giving rather than getting. We do not want to forgive our torturers as Jesus does (see Luke 23:34), so we ignore the perspective and way of being that Jesus offers and instead create a Christianity that answers our question, namely: "How do we go to heaven and avoid going to hell?" That certainly sells better than the ontological truth Jesus offers—but, interestingly, that question has had a great variety of answers over the years, and still does.

For the early church, going to heaven was not a pressing question since most believed Jesus would be returning within their lifetime. Once a few generations had passed, the question of heaven and how to get there became an issue. As the church became more established, a system of sacraments and theologies began to form, but they still did not give us an answer to who was in and who was out in terms of heaven. With the Protestant Reformation, there was a new emphasis on Scripture due to the invention of moveable type. Books had suddenly become available, and Protestants became the people of the Book. With the Reformation, there was also a new emphasis on faith, which eventually came to mean believing the right theology based upon a particular perspective and reading of the Scripture. Faith had begun as the great mystery of which Jesus spoke, but, by the twentieth century, many Christians saw faith as a matter of being certain about the doctrines they trusted for salvation.

Christian theology and doctrines have certainly changed over time, just as the way we think and talk about the world changes over time. For example, the ancient world understood bizarre human behavior as demonic possession. Today we explain the same behavior as a psychotic disorder like schizophrenia. Literalists believe these are two phenomena rather than two different perspectives on the same thing. To believe they are different entities is to confuse the theory or perspective with the thing itself. Scientists still discuss whether light is of a wave or a corpuscular nature, but they do not believe they are talking about two different things, merely two different ways of talking about the same thing. Jesus used the vernacular and perspective of his day. No other language or perspective was available, or would have been understood, but whether he cast out demons or cured schizophrenia is impossible to say. Jesus healed a person, but there is no way to know if the event and our way of talking about the event are identical. To believe that they are identical is to believe that language mirrors reality rather than simply being our way of talking about our experience. Perhaps demonic possession and schizophrenia are two different matters and not simply two different perspectives on the same thing, but to think that they are entirely different simply because there are two different ways of talking about bizarre behavior is to confuse our perspective with the thing itself.

W HAT WE KNOW and how we express what we know changes with our changing perspectives and the vicissitudes of history. Such changes do not affect our transformation into Jesus' truth, however, since Jesus' truth is not an epistemic truth that we simply know and believe. We experience transformation into his likeness, not by what we know and believe, but by falling in love with the things that Jesus said and did because we recognize them as divinely beautiful and good. What we fall in love with determines who we are, and falling in love with the things that Jesus said and did is what begins to make us into his likeness. If you believe all the facts about Jesus' life, but do not think that loving your enemy or giving without expecting anything in return is divinely beautiful, you do not know the truth of which Jesus spoke. Transformation into his likeness begins by falling in love with the things he said and did because we recognize them as divinely beautiful and good, not simply because we think they are true. Once we have fallen in love with the beauty and goodness of Jesus' words and deeds, we seek to emulate his constant awareness of the divine presence, his forgiveness to all who ask, and his mercy to an undeserving world.

Of course, most people prefer a Christianity that is simply a matter of believing the right theological doctrines. Such truths sell much better than following Jesus into the kind of being to which he calls us. Furthermore, most people justify their refusal to follow Jesus by claiming that "He was Divine" and therefore we cannot be as Jesus was. That seems to make sense, but it rests upon a notion of righteousness that is very different from that to which Jesus calls us. Many Christians think that righteousness is either a matter of right beliefs or the avoidance of what their culture tells them is sin. Jesus, however, speaks of a righteousness that comes through repentance. Not that repentance makes us righteous, but repentance opens us to the experience of God's mercy, and it is the ongoing experience of God's mercy, for having failed to live as Jesus lived, that eventually makes us into his merciful likeness. Those who are "forgiven little, love little" (see Luke 7:47) and those who realize how much mercy they have received become merciful. Following Jesus into the truth to which he calls us is not about becoming righteous or sinless, as he is sinless, but about becoming merciful, as he is merciful.

Jesus prayed that his church would be one (see John 17:20–22), but many people's idea of Christianity as a matter of knowing and believing the right doctrines, practicing the right rituals, and abstaining from the sins that their culture believes to be most grievous, has separated Christians into over forty thousand denominations worldwide. The only doctrinal truth that has the power to unite us in order to realize Jesus' prayer is the truth of our common and universal failure to be as Jesus calls us to be. Likewise, the only behavior that has the power to unite us is a repentance that leads into the perpetual experience of God's mercy.   •

The Heart of Deep Change

By David G. Benner

PEOPLE SOMETIMES SMILE when I tell them that I work as a transformational coach. I think I understand why the notion of trying to facilitate transformation might seem laughable. If such things as eating less or exercising more are as notoriously difficult as most of us realize, what hope could there ever be for the sort of quantum change that is implied by the notion of transformation? Perhaps the cynicism of the fable of the frog and the scorpion is justified.

> One day, a scorpion wanted to cross a river. However, he couldn't swim. Seeing a frog sitting on the bank, he asked the frog to carry him across the river on his back. The frog refused. "I don't trust you," he said. "I know how dangerous scorpions are. If you get on my back, you'll sting and kill me." The scorpion answered, "Why would I do that? If I sting you, we'll both drown." "But how do I know you won't kill me when we get to

the other side?" asked the frog. The scorpion replied, "I would never do that because I will be too grateful for your help to ever sting you." After thinking about this for a minute, the frog agreed to let the scorpion get on his back. He began swimming, gradually feeling safer and safer, even starting to think he had been silly to worry. But, halfway across the river, the scorpion suddenly stung the frog. "You fool," croaked the frog, "Now we will both die! Why did you do that?" The scorpion answered, "Because I'm a scorpion. It's my nature to sting."

The possibilities of changing human nature seem equally unrealistic, nor does it appear that there is much chance of changing the basic framework of our personality. We all go through life dealing with a small number of very personal struggles, vulnerabilities, and besetting predispositions, and nothing short of death seems to fully deliver us from them.

Transformation occurs at a quite different level of our being. The seat of transformational change is consciousness. Fortunately, profound changes in consciousness subsequently lead to profound changes in identity, which then tend to ripple out into other dimensions of our being. Changing the platform from which we view and experience life is very powerful and that is the reason consciousness lies at the heart of transformation.

NORMAL WAKING CONSCIOUSNESS

To UNDERSTAND the way in which we can facilitate the transformation of consciousness, we must first briefly consider normal waking consciousness. We can get a snapshot by noticing what is going on within us as we prepare to fall asleep. Most people first become aware of thoughts: of the present and recent days, about upcoming events, about their feelings, about their bodies, and much more. Thoughts keep us awake at night and also, paradoxically, keep us from truly awakening. In both cases, this reflects our attachment, not so much to specific thoughts as to normal waking consciousness.

Paying attention to the contents of consciousness might, of course, make us aware of other things beyond thoughts. We might, for example, notice a song or fragment of music that is part of our waking

Awareness is *presence to what is.*

consciousness, or perhaps it is pain or anxiety that lurks on the edges of awareness. But, once we notice these sorts of things, we tend to create thoughts about them. Consequently, thoughts remain central to waking consciousness for most people.

But notice I speak of *becoming aware* of thoughts and other things. Thoughts are not awareness. They arise from awareness. Awareness is *presence to what is.* Thoughts are what the mind creates to express *what seems to be.* They are our judgments about the things that arise in awareness. This is why thoughts create duality. Awareness is non-dual, like the ocean. Thoughts are like the ocean's waves—ripples on the surface of the whole.

Thoughts are mental construals that point toward reality. Sadly, however, we easily confuse them with reality. All thoughts and words are but fingers pointing to the moon. Unfortunately, most people confuse the moon with the finger and never get around to directly experiencing the reality behind the words. This is why meditation offers tremendously important help in cultivating ways of softening our attachment to thoughts, something that is essential if we are to experience authentic transformation.

THE TRANSFORMATION OF CONSCIOUSNESS

TRANSFORMATION OF CONSCIOUSNESS involves much more than the mere production of an altered state of consciousness. That is relatively easy to do since we cycle through such states on a daily basis. By transformation, I mean an enduring *expansion* of consciousness that expresses itself in increased awareness; a broader, more inclusive identity; and a larger framework for meaning-making. Together, these things result in a changed way of experiencing and being in the world. This is what I would call really deep change.

Thoughts are what the mind creates to express *what seems to be.*

Make no mistake about it: Transformation is a serious threat to institutional religion—Christianity certainly included. The release of control that is essential if a community is to genuinely support—not just talk about—transformation is seriously subversive to the maintenance of communities built around belief and belonging. Transformation does require communal support, but that support must be free of constraint. This is why, as Richard Rohr notes, most religion is more tribal than transformational.[1]

Before looking at how we can genuinely support transformation, let us go back for just a moment to normal waking consciousness. Recall the central place thoughts have in it. This is why it is common to describe the default level of consciousness as mental. The primary contents of consciousness—thoughts—are products of the mind. But also, noticing how self-referential most of these thoughts typically are tells us how egoic this level of consciousness-development is. Our background preoccupation reflects our small ego-self. We may talk, think, write, and teach about the larger horizons of the unfolding self, but it is deceptively easy to do so from the egoic, mental stage of consciousness development.[2]

Thankfully, this is not the only way in which consciousness can be organized. Consciousness can be transformed and its deep center can shift from our minds to our hearts. There is much more involved in transformation,[3] but this shift from our heads to our hearts brings us to the heart of the process.

In the wisdom tradition, the heart is understood as the fullness of the mind. Its resources include, but are never limited to, the mind. It contains a range of other subtle, usually underdeveloped faculties such as imagination, intuition, and symbolic communication. The heart senses wholes, "gets" poetry and art, and gives us our expansiveness—stretching out beyond our individuality to connect us to the very heart of the universe. Unlike ego, the heart doesn't perceive by differentiation, but by means of its inherent resonance with alignment, oneness, harmony, proportion, and beauty. The egoic mind creates and thrives on dualism. The heart throbs with resonance to the integral wholeness that exists in and beyond itself, and to which it calls us.

HEARTFUL WAYS OF FACILITATING TRANSFORMATION

NOTHING ARISING FROM within the egoic self can be of much help in facilitating transformation. No problem can be solved from the same level of consciousness that created it. This is the limitation of trying to facilitate transformation through books and lectures that primarily engage the mind. No matter how much you speak *of* the heart, if you are speaking *to* the mind it will never be received in a truly transformational way. Speaking to the mind simply reinforces attachment to the mind and normal waking consciousness.

Welcoming Awakenings

AWAKENING ALWAYS STARTS with the heart. The mind may experience insights but, unless this leads to the awakening of the heart, insights will never be truly transformational. Responding to an awakening with openness and emptiness is a heartful expression of consent to the transformational action of Spirit within our depths.

A Sufi story succinctly describes the role of awakening in transformation:

Disciple: What can I do to make myself enlightened?
Teacher: As little as you can do to make the sun rise in the morning.
Disciple: Then of what use are spiritual practices?
Teacher: They help ensure you are not asleep when the sun begins to rise.

There is nothing we can do to engineer either the awakening or transformation. Our role is simply to respond with consent to the invitations to awakening that life brings us. We offer this consent through our openness and emptiness. This seems totally counter-intuitive to the egoic mind, which focuses on creating and maintaining fullness as a defense against the unbearable lightness and emptiness of being. But it is the path to transformation. The heart thrives in the spaciousness of emptiness and invites us to let go of all the things that fill us up and weigh us down.

Embracing Silence

SILENT RETREATS have played an important role in Christian spiritual formation and transformation for two millennia. Jesus modeled them through his proclivity for regular times of wilderness retreat and the Desert Fathers and Mothers followed him into the deserts of Egypt and Syria a couple of centuries later. Many of us have followed this call to embrace silence and discover the disruptive way in which it forces us out of normal waking consciousness. It is not uncommon to see this level of disruptiveness reach such intolerable levels among first-time retreatants that some feel forced to escape the distress by leaving the retreat. Those who stay differ from them, not by an absence of the disruption, but by their consent to the invitation of Spirit to step into the liminal space that silence evokes.

Sadly, silent retreats have increasingly given way to teaching retreats with blocks of silence, and these have then given way to teaching conferences with pauses to stretch your legs so you can continue to fill yourself up with content. Silence should not be seen as emptying that is intended to make you more available for subsequent filling. Silence is emptying. Only this prepares you for transformation. Engaging silence in this way requires skillful accompaniment. This is the important role of a spiritual guide in a directed retreat.

Clearly there is great potential value in teaching, with or without silence. But information broadcasting is not in itself transformational and new information is far from necessary to make use of silence. In fact, information usually contaminates the field by being, at best, a distraction and, at worst, diminishing the transformational potential by reinforcing ordinary waking consciousness. Silence and solitude prepare us for transformation by opening access to the heart that simply is not available in normal waking consciousness.

Engaging Imagination

I WAS FORTUNATE to grow up in a family and church that introduced me to the importance of daily periods of silence before God and regular periods of more extended retreat. Unfortunately, however, I quickly found a way to defend against their transformational potential. Because my attachment to my thoughts was so strong, I was

The value of intuition lies precisely in the fact that it is so different from reason.

very happy to use silence as time for thinking. This, of course, simply strengthened my egoic self.

I am sure I also could have successfully sabotaged my engagement with the Ignatian Spiritual Exercises, but it was the central role of the imagination that made it such a turning point in my life. I was aware of the potential disruptiveness of work with the imagination and, because of this, had resisted engaging with the Ignatian Spiritual Exercises for many years—even after my wife, Juliet, completed her training as an Ignatian spiritual director. I told her that I suspected I'd fail at anything that put so much emphasis on the imagination. She smiled and told me that was precisely why I needed to engage them—when I was ready!

When I was ready, by far the most powerful part of the experience was the daily imaginal conversations I had with Jesus, Mary, Joseph, and other figures in the Gospel stories. It was during a conversation with the young child Jesus that I had the most powerful awakening of my life. In the midst of our conversation, I suddenly heard three words: "Withdraw from love." The words had nothing to do with the conversation I was having with Jesus, nor with anything I had been consciously thinking about, but instantly I knew what they meant. They pointed to resentment I had first felt at age four when I suddenly had to share my mother with a new baby brother—a resentment of which I had no previous awareness, despite years of dream- and other forms of soul-work and personal psychotherapy. They also nailed my way of defending against my resentment by withdrawing from my mother's freely given love, choosing instead to work toward earning her respect. This wasn't merely an insight. It moved quickly from my mind to my heart in an awakening that eventually led to profound changes in my consciousness and life.

Ignatian spirituality is undoubtedly not the only Christian tradition that makes use of the imagination. Nor is the imagination the only way to get out of the mind and into the deeper regions of the heart. Anything that causes even momentary disruption to ordinary waking consciousness has the potential to be a portal through which a person may receive invitations to awaken.

Nurturing Intuition

ONE FEATURE of the heart that makes it particularly threatening to the mind is its subjectivity. From the perspective of the egoic mind, the heart is a messy soup of fuzzy-mindedness that cannot be trusted because it can't be engaged with objectivity. Nowhere is this felt to be truer than with intuition.

All of us know something of our intuitive capacities, but most of us have been sufficiently discouraged from trusting them that they remain seriously underdeveloped. Yet the value of intuition lies precisely in the fact that it is so different from reason. It should never be expected to replace careful thought. But, when disciplined by deepening connections between head and heart and engaged with discernment, intuition offers a tremendously important way to access deep wisdom.

One of the ways I teach people to engage with and eventually trust their intuition is by encouraging them to pay attention to their subjectivity. Usually, when I address groups, I suggest that, instead of listening primarily to my words, they should attend principally to the movements within their hearts as their minds process what I have to share. Some people refuse to do this because they are afraid they will miss something important. It is just too hard to believe that what they most need in the moment will be heard without effort, and that paying primary attention to their subjective experience will add immeasurably to the value of what is heard because it will deepen their engagement with it. I used to regularly do the same in psychotherapy and spiritual direction, and now make it a routine part of my transformational coaching conversations. I also take my own advice. This means that, in dialogue, each of us is attending both to the other and to our own deep self. And, of course, in listening to our own deep self, we are attending to the One who is with us, and whose presence makes our presence to each other possible.

THESE ARE A FEW of the many available means to move out of our minds and into our hearts. The use of music, dance, and other creative expressions should also be included in any list of such ways. For many years, my wife and I have led silent retreats built around guided engagement with art and poetry.[4] The people who are the most deeply impacted are always the ones who protest that they don't "get" either art or poetry. That doesn't matter. What does matter is that they allow those things to open their hearts.

All it takes for those of us who seek to facilitate awakening and transformation is to avoid reinforcing the typical ways people use to defend against awakening. This simply means that we avoid engaging them primarily through their default level of consciousness. Whenever we help people open their hearts, not simply their minds, we bring them to the threshold of awakening and deep change. With that, we have done all we can do. •

The Bell Rack of My Selfhood

By Cynthia Bourgeault

OVER THESE PAST TWO decades of spiritual teaching, I have found myself increasingly bumping up against the hard edges of two core assumptions that frame the way most of us understand transformation.

The first is the assumption that spirituality is an *ascent*, with its dominant metaphor of the *ladder*. The way to God is "up," and the most keenly sought-after spiritual states are described as "higher." Like all ladders, the goal is to get to the top.

The second is the pervasive habit of setting up the journey in terms of an *interior combat*, with the mortal enemy typically identified as the "ego" or "false self," a distorted but tenacious part of our own selfhood. This assumption drives the widespread use of the metaphor of *spiritual warfare*, where the goal of transformation is to vanquish, silence, "dismantle," or override that lower self which, in the words of *The Course in Miracles*, "wants you dead."

Now, the one thing I've learned over these years of spiritual seeking is the deep wisdom to be gleaned from a celebrated assertion attributed to the Mad Hatter: "How you get there is where you'll arrive." The two master metaphors of axial spirituality (ascent and combat) set us down in a spiritual terrain marked by oppositionality (a.k.a. *duality*), judgment, competitiveness, and, implicitly (sometimes *explicitly*), violence. If spiritual transformation is fundamentally about growth, mere common sense tells us that this is not the optimal environment for things to grow. The path of "internal warfare" has certainly produced its spiritual heroes, but has also reaped more than its share of vainglory, repression, self-righteousness, and fear.

Is there a kinder and gentler way of framing transformation?

As I pondered this question, I soon discovered that the alternative metaphor was literally ringing in my ears. Many years ago, when I spent a season of my life as an ecumenical fellow at St John's Abbey, that great Benedictine mother-ship nestled on a lakeside in rural Minnesota, my ears soon became attuned to the clamor of the great bell rack that erupted periodically throughout the day. Over the entrance to the imposing, Marcel Breuer-designed Abbey Church stood an enormous concrete bell banner housing five bells of different sizes and timbres (none of them less than one thousand pounds, I'd guess; we are talking *massive* here!).

Several times a day, but with particular gusto right before daily mass at 5:00 p.m., the grand hullabaloo would begin. One bell would get rolling, then the others would join in their turn, until finally the whole countryside was enfolded in a single, sonorous tapestry. Then gradually the order would reverse; one by one, the bells dropped away until only the single announcing bell remained. Then it, too, fell silent and the liturgy commenced. Throughout the entire year at St. John's, I never grew tired of those bells, which always seemed to be calling me back to something deeper inside myself, something more numinous and whole.

There it was, I realized—my alternative metaphor for selfhood: the *bell rack*! Not a higher self and lower self, locked in mortal combat; not a merciless race to the spiritual top; but a family of different sizes, shapes, and timbres, all contributing their unique melody to the whole.

I will shortly introduce each of the four bells in my bell rack and explain a bit more about how this alternative metaphor works, but first let me fill in one more key piece of the backstory. A major turning point in my own journey of transformation came about twenty years ago, in the course of some very intense shadow work

Nafs is really our *protector*-self—and, what's more, in a strange but real way, the reciprocal measure of our capacity for transformation.

undertaken with my beloved jousting partner, Brother Raphael Robin.

Prior to that time, as a good student of Centering Prayer, I had been patiently working to dismantle my false self, assuming that my "true self" would be what was left when the illusory pretender was exposed. But, as the raw intimacy of the work with Rafe intensified, we both began to notice that it was not the best side of ourselves that God seemed to be calling forth in the crucible of transformation, but, strangely, the *worst*—maybe because that's where the seeds of our redeemed essence were, in fact, planted. My desperate clinging and grasping that so dogged the path of our relationship would eventually reemerge in the transforming fires as an authentic capacity for devotion. His towering isolation turned out to guard the threshold to an almost unbearably tender compassion. Throw out the bathwater, and out goes the baby with it!

THROUGH THE WORK with Rafe, I gradually came to see that the much-maligned "false self" is really our *protector*-self—and, what's more, in a strange but real way, the reciprocal measure of our capacity for transformation. When you think about it, it's extraordinary to what lengths a vulnerable and wounded human being will go, what intricate psychic armor he or she will construct, in order to remain in the game of life. In that sense, this *nafs* (as the Sufis call it), this "lower, passional self," really carries the force of our *hope*, our stubborn courage to hang in, even when the odds seem hopelessly stacked against us. The goal, then, is not to dismantle it, but to *transfigure* it, reclaiming the qualities of essence it has so valiantly defended. That recognition was a huge turning point in my own spiritual journey, a whole new way of looking at myself and others.

Consequently, in my bell rack, I do indeed call the first bell my *nafs*, my lower, passional self. I prefer this to the term "false self," for there is absolutely nothing false about *nafs* (except in comparison to some hypothetical "true self"). It is empirically real. It is an ancient and familiar part of our being—and it is not our enemy. *Nafs* is our functional storefront for dealing with the issues of the world, meeting life head-on, and keeping things moving along the horizontal axis. Also, typically, until we have extensive spiritual work under our belt, it is the principal source of our *personal agency*; nothing much is going to get done in our lives without its cooperation.

The second bell in my bell rack I call *soul*. Soul is the voice of the artist and lover in me, the cosmic gambler, the Delphic oracle who believes that, beneath the shifting sands of daily life, there is a deeper pattern at work, a truer version of who I am, waiting patiently to be discovered. Soul speaks to us in a thousand voices: in dreams and archetypes, in shades of value, in the richness of the emotive life, in the siren call to authenticity. There is always an aspect of hidden-ness here; she must be discovered and teased out from among the thousand mirages of *nafs*-ordered life. But when we get her right, it is always with that rich sense of coming round to where we began and "know[ing] the place for the first time."[1]

Soul is the true feeling of myself *from the perspective of my finite selfhood*—or, in other words, as viewed through the lens of my self-reflective consciousness. It is the deepest and truest story of me. But it is, in the end, a *story*: the reflected light of something far more allusive and real, to which it points through the hall of mirrors of my *faculties*, that is to say, my memory, reason, imagination, feeling, and will.

Spirit is seamless and indivisible; it really belongs only to God.

The third bell in my bell rack I call *spirit*. But, in fact, this is not really "my" bell at all; it does not belong to "me." Spirit is seamless and indivisible; it really belongs only to God. As it enters our being (at conception), it turns on the lights of our individual animation and dwells within us as the animating principle and the specific reminder of that which is infinite within us. Sometimes it floods us with drenching downloads of unboundaried consciousness: "I am *that*," I exclaim. But truly, we will never "become" spirit. It dwells in us and, through that indwelling, connects us to the formless—and the formbound to itself. To paraphrase that old cliché, it is the Divine having a human experience.

Heart is my last bell. Here things get a bit more complicated, for heart shares many traits with soul, yet has a distinctly different flavor. If soul is the sense of myself generated through my finite operating system—i.e., through *reflecting* on my being—heart is what happens when I simply and purely *coincide* with my being, when the ocean enters the drop. The view is holographic rather than linear; there are still specific essence qualities to my being, but they do not *define* me, let alone differentiate me from others. Comparison/contrast has dropped out.

Heart is concrete, particular, practical, often surprising. Unlike soul, it is not insistent or fussy. Its wellbeing does not depend on fulfilling a specific set of external conditions; rather, it comes roaring in from the infinite, filling every nook and cranny of any and all conditions with the fullness of its being. It is the lion in winter in the cave of my heart, and when it wakes up and begins to roar, the whole bell rack explodes in a single harmonic offering.

It is also the true seat of the *personal*—or, in other words, of the dynamic, relational aliveness that emerges when my being is entirely "sounded through" ("*per-sonare*") by my *true*, true self, which does not belong to this earthly plane. As Black Elk would say, it is "the shadow cast on earth from yonder vision in the heaven, so bright it was, so clear."[2] As the Sufis would say, heart is the angel of my Being.

I SPOKE EARLIER ABOUT those two master metaphors that tend to frame our understanding of transformation. To this I would now like to add a third metaphor, closely related to the other two and, in fact, their corollary: the belief that the purpose of our sojourn here on earth is to earn admission to somewhere else, somewhere better. Call it heaven, nirvana, the non-dual realm—the name does not matter;

the bottom line is the same. Again and again, that Neoplatonic siren call of "spiritualization" (the ladder, ready at hand) seduces us onward and upward again, away from the simple, incarnational epicenter of our Christian faith: "for God so *loved* the world that he gave his only son..." (see John 3:16).

But if we really come back to center and view our world through Christ-focused eyes, we come to see that this earthly plane is not a waiting room for heaven or a final exam to see if we qualify; it is the place where certain aspects of love, which can only be spoken in form and finitude, are indeed spoken, resonating simultaneously through all realms, visible and invisible. I am thinking here about qualities such as fidelity, steadfastness, and most particularly what I call *Eucharistic love*: the capacity to have your heart broken wide open without resorting to despair or bitterness. These are subtle essences of love that can only be woven on the warp of time and the weft of finitude, but they are the most intimate love song at the heart of our Common Father—"the treasure longing to be known," as the Sufis call it—and it is our tremendous privilege and honor, here on this earthly plane, to be able to play that love song on the lute strings of our own heart.

Funny, isn't it, how we spend most of our spiritual energy trying to get out of human form when the real goal of existence is actually to get *into* it.

ONE WAY OR ANOTHER, it seems beyond dispute that our composite human psyche seems to be perfectly anatomically wired for the job of mediating between the infinite and the finite, the universal and the particular, the gross world of form and the more subtle realms, in a marvelous and mysterious two-way street—almost as if it were deliberately set up that way. In this mysterious cosmic assignment, if that's what it is, the finite parts of our selfhood are as vital and indispensable as our high-soaring spiritual yearnings, and the tension between these two perspectives must not be collapsed, but rather consciously borne. As that late, great wise woman Helen Luke once famously remarked, "Wholeness is born of the acceptance of the conflict of human and divine in the individual psyche."[3]

Not suppression of the conflict, but *acceptance* of it, as part of the sacred task of being a human being—if that's your map of transformation, as it has become mine, then the goal is to welcome *all* the voices, all perspectives, all the blessed ways in which we spontaneously hold dual citizenship in both the finite and the formless realms. Rooted and grounded in both, we do our best to live here worthily and with gusto, to bless and upload the fruits of our finitude directly into the divine heart—which is not "up," incidentally, but rather "*all*": the entire cosmic bell rack.

And so, speaking of bell racks, I can only end by yielding the floor to Leonard Cohen, whose vision almost perfectly encapsulates what I understand about transformation:

> Ring the bells that still can ring
> Forget your perfect offering
> There is a crack in everything
> That's how the light gets in.[4]

Four
Shapes to
Transformation

By Richard Rohr

BUILDING ON WHAT I wrote in my short introduction to this edition of *Oneing*, I would like to give our theme of transformation four very specific meanings, at least as they apply to the human spiritual journey. I am inspired by the very simple and clarifying language used by Ken Wilber in a recent dialogue I had with him in Denver, but will also be offering my own understandings of the same.

Wilber's Four Transformations are cleverly described as *Growing Up, Waking Up, Cleaning Up,* and *Showing Up*. Only in the fourth transformation do I take a largely different direction than Wilber—without disagreeing with him at all! Let me give you a short description of all four transformations and how they interact—and also interfere with and build upon one another.

GROWING UP

G ROWING UP refers to the process of psychological and emotional maturity that persons commonly undergo, both personally and culturally (Wilber and I both rely upon the comprehensive schema called Spiral Dynamics for this trajectory). We mature personally, yet that maturity also reflects our own period of history, our culture, our family, and our social class's values and assumptions. We mirror one another. We all grow up, but inside our own bubbles. The social structures that surround us highly color, strengthen, and also limit how much we can grow up and how much of our own shadow self we will be able to face and integrate. (We will see shortly that growing up, to a large degree, has to do with "cleaning up" or facing our various shadow issues.)

To give a central Christian example, even Jesus and Paul, although we would assume they were psychologically and emotionally mature, were still limited by their period of history and their first-century assumptions. A complete assault on the universally assumed phenomena of slavery or patriarchy would have been both impossible for them to imagine and largely unhearable by others. They still had to take their place in the evolution of consciousness, as we all must do.

Nevertheless, Jesus has largely been interpreted throughout history by much less mature minds than his, and his teachings have stretched us much farther than most of his followers were ready to go. We must humbly accept that twentieth-century pluralistic, democratic, egalitarian consciousness (the "green level" of Spiral Dynamics) was beyond most people's reach until very recently—and Jesus was leading us even beyond that! He did, however, *fully lay the theological foundation for the dismantling of patriarchy and autocracy, and for the full understanding of an egalitarian world of equal dignity.* (Hold onto this idea as we explore the other levels of transformation.)

It is important to note that personal growth and cultural growth are not the same thing. It is common for a culture to be quite "grown up" and yet for an individual to remain immature inside of that nation, church, era, or ethnicity. That hardly needs to be proven. On the other end of the spectrum, Mohandas Gandhi and Nelson Mandela grew up personally and far surpassed their culture's common level of maturity. Such people represent the cutting edge of how much human transformation is really possible—and where it is heading. They usually end up as either prophets or martyrs, or both.

What a gift it is for those who are able to grow up personally but also have their society to support, educate, and understand them. I think that is what I enjoyed in my own formative years in the 1960s. "To be young was very heaven," as Wordsworth put it, speaking of the period of the French Revolution.[1] Such people can either be the cutting edge of the next age of civilization, or use their privileged awareness for their own private advancement—which is not to be very grown-up at all! Surely this is why Jesus had so many warnings about privilege, pride, and consumerism. Any full growing-up has to be a growing *outward* and not just upward; in other words, *you can be aware without being caring*—which is not to be very aware! (In the Franciscan school of philosophy and theology, this was stated as love being a larger and higher virtue or quality than knowledge.)

WAKING UP

B
Y "WAKING UP," we are speaking of *any spiritual experience which overcomes our experience of the self as separate from Being in general.* This is variously referred to as enlightenment, supreme awareness, awakening, *satori,* and unitive consciousness, and it should be the full Christian meaning of salvation. Unfortunately, we pushed all waking up into something that would hopefully happen later, in heaven or after death, or as a reward for good behavior in this world. This was a major loss and defeat for Christianity and a disastrous misplacement of attention. *We became a religion of religious transactions more than spiritual transformation.* It led to an almost magical notion of sacraments if you were Orthodox or Catholic and an almost juridical understanding of Bible quotes and moral positions if you were Protestant.

Waking up should be the final goal of all spiritual work, sacraments, and Bible study, but, at least in the West, this has not been the case. Because we were not *practice-based* for the most part, and had a bias against inner experience, it seemed very presumptuous to actually believe—or believe possible—the conclusion of every significant mystic: Jesus' "I and the Father are one" (see John 10:30), Augustine's "God is closer to me than I am to myself," or Catherine of Genoa's "My

Waking up
should be the final goal
of all spiritual work, sacraments,
and Bible study, but, at least in the
West, this has not been the case.

deepest me is God." *Organized Christianity largely described waking up in terms of growing up, and that growing up was almost entirely interpreted in highly moralistic terms —and even that morality was largely culturally defined!* Please read that twice; it might be the most pertinent point for most of us.

Now, of course, this unitive experience of the self is what Jesus is referring to as "the vine and the branches" experience (see John 15:5). It is quite an exact metaphor for the shape of Christian *holiness*, but we settled for a much smaller definition of psychological or moral wholeness—at which no one ever felt they fully succeeded. Most gave up, or did not even try, with the glaring evidence of their humanity shouting loudly and insistently from every side.

Most of Western Christianity failed to offer people an ontological, theological, objective basis for holiness, which was, of course, the fully implanted *imago Dei* (see Genesis 1:26–27 and Romans 5:5), and has nothing to do with moral perfection or psychological wholeness—but totally precedes and grounds all our successes and failures. In short, Western religions have not done waking up very well, but that does not mean God did not keep on working, in spite of our limited theology of the very nature of salvation—which is entirely a gift and never an achievement (see Ephesians 2:8–10).

The good news is that saints, mystics, and holy people still emerged everywhere. Lots of people woke up—frankly, almost in spite of the dominant consciousness. When it did happen, it was usually through *great love and great suffering*, much more than through any direct ministry of ministers. The Scriptures and the writings of the mystics were always there to support them, but there were invariably few authoritative interpreters and motivators to help them or guide them in waking up. Most ministers were satisfied with trying to get people to "clean up"! Yet, even there, we kept our God-carrot on a long stick, far out in front of any would-be seeker.

CLEANING UP

W E MINISTERS TALKED, wrote, and preached about "cleaning up" the most, but actually did this very poorly. Religion was almost exclusively identified with morality (They are not the same, as such; mature morality is a corollary of religious encounter.), not any deep transformation of consciousness. We largely reflected the moral preoccupations of the dominant culture in every age and every denomination. We surely reminded people of their moral failings, tried to clean them up from their seemingly "hot sins"—Protestants with "fire and brimstone" sermons and Catholics with regular shaming and reminders of mortal sin and confession. Despite Jesus' brilliant and to-the-point teaching on "the splinter in your neighbor's eye and the log in your own" (see Matthew 7:3–5), we only developed the word and concept of the "shadow self" in the last hundred years—and even now it is not commonly understood.

It took very honest and non-ideological groups like Alcoholics Anonymous and much of modern therapy to bring "cleaning up" down to earth. As you know, our shadow self is what we do not want to see about ourselves, so we deny it, and hate it in other people. We *project our rejected self onto others and reject them instead!* We usually do not have the strength to see this until after a few moral failures, and often not until the second half of life. It just takes too much honesty and an immense humility, plus patience over time.

Our largely external understanding of morality was very superficial and reflected our not-so-grown-up culture's values, bound to our time in history and seldom driven by the brilliance of Jesus' moral ideals, which are, *first of all,* inner and attitudinal (see Matthew 6–7)—in other words, a change in consciousness itself. The emphases of Christian morality also changed every century or so, from disbelief to riches, to warfare, to non-conformity, to usury, to doctrinal heresy, to disobedience, to "commerce" with other religions, to sexuality/

embodiment in almost every form, to our contemporary preoccupation with abortion and homosexuality.

Cleaning up also changed a lot in determining what *purity* or goodness really is, and it invariably reflected the shadow side of each culture. The Germans, like myself, were afraid of disorder and tardiness; the English were afraid of being improper or expressive; the Spaniards of being vulnerable or egalitarian; and much of the world feared being considered dirty, small, or unintelligent. We all had our unique shame base. Starting with the Law of Holiness (see Leviticus 16–25), moral goodness had much more to do with *separation from impure things, people, and places* than with *separation from our egoic and small selves*, which is what both Jesus and the Buddha clearly and directly talked about.

This endless need for purity is what Catholic spirituality called the "purgative stage" of spirituality (now called "Recovery"), but because we did it so poorly and in such a very limited way, most people never moved beyond early purgation to the "illuminative stage" of really growing up, much less set out on the "unitive way" of waking up. In short, *Christianity became a moralistic phenomenon instead of a mystical phenomenon*, which has lasted to this day. People will still ask me, "Can Catholics do this?" or "Are Christians forbidden to do that?" This is a very bad starting place and an even worse ending place.

We do indeed need to clean up, but this is largely an issue of putting boundaries to our natural egocentricity, which does have the potential to wake us up to our separateness over time. *The goal in waking up is not personal or private perfection, but surrender, love, and union with God.* Any preoccupation with my private moral perfection keeps my eyes on myself and not on God or grace or love. Cleaning up is largely about the need for early impulse control and creating necessary ego boundaries—so you can actually show up in the real and much bigger world.

SHOWING UP

F INALLY, KEN WILBER uses the term "showing up" to refer to honoring all four "quadrants" of his comprehensive integral schema, the individual interior (I), the individual exterior (behavior), the collective interior (culture), and the collective exterior (society). It makes a lot of sense, and I would strongly encourage any-

Showing up means bringing our heart and mind into the actual suffering and problems of the world.

one to become "integral" and show up in all four quadrants of reality. But I also suspect that most people on this earth will never think this through—or even need to think it through. For most of us, it will be presented and learned much more simply and intuitively.

For me, *showing up means bringing our heart and mind into the actual suffering and problems of the world*. It means engagement, social presence, and a sincere concern for justice and peace—and others beyond ourselves. It means having the courage to enter the fray of life and even being willing to make big mistakes or appear foolish enough to do so. This is why some philosophers have said that courage is finally the foundation of all the other virtues. Low-level virtue is largely about looking good to others; sincere virtue is caring about others.

So showing up is the full and final result of cleaning up, growing up, and waking up. It is God's fully transformed "work of art" (see Ephesians 2:10). If we do not have a lot of people showing up in the suffering trenches of the world, it is probably because those of us in the world of religion have allowed them to stop with merely cleaning up, growing up, or waking up.

Many tried to grow up, but never faced their personal or cultural shadow.

Many tried to clean up, without recognizing the necessity of having any goal beyond that.

Many have awakened for a while (in the midst of great love and great suffering, or even their own burning-bush experience), but they were unable to undertake the mundane work of cleaning up and growing up, so they went back to sleep.

Full spiritual transformation is a runway, lying ahead of us and open to all (beyond denominationalism). Few generations have been offered so many skillful tools and teachers to undertake all four transformations in one lifetime.

We are that generation. •

The Unfolding Story of the Universe:

A Conversation with Mary Evelyn Tucker and Julianne Warren

By Sam Mowe

In their Journey of the Universe project —which includes a film, book, and website —philosopher Brian Thomas Swimme and historian of religions Mary Evelyn Tucker attempt to tell the biggest story ever told: the history of the universe. Through a compelling blend of scientific facts and humanistic inquiry, they move from exploring the formation of the galaxies, stars, planets, and evolution of life on Earth to reflecting on the role of humanity during our current moment of social and ecological challenges.

One person whose work has been deeply influenced by the Journey of the Universe project is writer and ecological thinker Julianne Warren. In her different projects exploring the Anthropocene, Warren has used Journey of the Universe as a touchstone while she asks questions about hope, transformation, and human responsibility.

Sam Mowe: Mary Evelyn, you've written that "the universe is not simply a place, it's a story." What do you mean by that?

Mary Evelyn Tucker: I'm suggesting that an unfolding narrative is one way of looking at the evolution of this fourteen-billion-year-old universe. Maybe the universe is best understood not as discrete incidents of evolution, but as a whole unfolding dynamic and developmental process, which is like a story. If you look at the universe as a place, it can feel a little bit static. Alternatively, we can begin to see ourselves as part of a dramatic story that's still unfolding and in which we have a part to play.

It's important to note that the understanding of evolution is only about 150 years old in human consciousness, since Darwin's *Origin of Species*. Developmental time is something human consciousness is just beginning to grasp. And, in a certain sense, this understanding allows us to be co-creators with this process.

Sam: How does understanding the universe as a story change our relationship with it?

Mary Evelyn: This epic story of evolution has an amazing potential to activate wonder, awe, and beauty that can sink into our bones and muscles. It's a story that can physically activate the energy of love for the beauty of ongoing life and the continuity of what's right in front of us. This possibility of activating a zest for life can give us the energy for doing the transformative work required to honor that beauty—whether it's conservation, education, political work, protest work, or whatever the realm is.

The deepest sources of human energy come from story. This past week, Peter Crane, the dean at the Yale School of Forestry and Environmental Studies, gave a talk on his life work on the history of angiosperms, namely flowering plants. He explained that these plants (of which there are over 250,000 species) have a history of some 145 million years. What paleobotanists are able to do now is actually unpack the fossil record and recreate—through the help of technology—the flowers, the pistil, the stems, and the rest. So he showed us this hundred-million-year-old flower bud, which was opening in this wonderful kinetic way, and it kept opening and opening and opening. It was completely riveting for the audience. It was one of the most spectacular things I've ever seen.

So now we're able to visualize the extraordinary power of deep time. There's an invitation here to think about how these species have emerged and changed over deep time.

Julianne Warren: Yes, I think that the way we integrate technology and creativity with our stories makes all the difference. The twentieth-century American literary ecologist, Aldo Leopold, observed a cultural cleavage in his best-selling book, A *Sand County Almanac*. In some peoples' stories, he explained, science is the sharpener of their swords. For others, science is a searchlight on their universe. In other words, science can help us invent tools for conquering land and each other. It can also stimulate humans' curiosity and wonder—as at the opening of an ancient flower bud—deepening our understandings and our skillful affection for all, as well as for appreciating mystery and our own ignorance.

Sam: There have been different cosmological stories told about the universe in various cultures around the world throughout history. One thing that makes the *Journey of the Universe* story different is that there is scientific evidence to back up the narrative. What do scientific facts add to the story?

Mary Evelyn: Scientific facts ground the story so that humans can enter into the creative processes of evolution. For example, the self-organizing dynamics of the universe that give rise to galaxies and stars stagger the mind and light up the imagination. And the imagination is what can connect us to understanding and interpreting these processes. So I think our challenge is to take the scientific knowledge and make it into wisdom, make it into something we can reflect on. When we look at pictures from the Hubble telescope, that's contemplation. You get the feeling of, "Wow, was I birthed out of these systems?" The stars really are our ancestors—literally and metaphorically.

Julianne: I would add that the rising understanding that humans have a large influence on the planet—its climate, soils, biodiversity, and so on—also presents a great irony. This is one irony of the Anthropocene: We can't control Earth the way we thought we could. The very science and technology that we applied to control the planet has revealed to us our inability to do so. And, we are, in a sense, trapped in the unintended, unwanted consequences of past human actions.

Another Anthropocene irony—one that unfetters us—is that while members of the dominating culture have considered themselves superior to the rest of nature and have tried to apply science and technology to set ourselves safely apart, what we are discovering is that we are inalienable. Though human influence is felt everywhere, human beings are embedded in a still-wild Earth. This means that we need to understand our mutual interdependencies better so that we can participate more generatively within the ecosphere.

Sam: This is interesting because initially I was thinking that you might be using scientific facts in *Journey of the Universe* as a strategic way to reach people, because many people take science more seriously than other modes of knowledge. Listening to you now it sounds like you're saying the scientific dimensions of the story, if told in a compelling way, have a special kind of power.

Mary Evelyn: Yes, that's right. It's worth pointing out that Brian Swimme and I took the science very seriously. This project was ten years in the making because we wanted to get the science right. We worked in the summers for a number of years with a group of scientists and we would go over different parts of the story. A number of scientists read the manuscript. The book was published in the science division of Yale University Press, and that's not easy. So the science is very tight in terms of its factual accuracy.

In each chapter there's a scientific fact. There's also a metaphor— such as the similarities between a whirlpool and our breath—that points toward meaning or how human beings fit in. So the scientific fact looked at metaphorically can capture the human imagination. From there, we explored ideas such as connectivity, relationality, and complex interdependence.

Julianne: Yes, this approach invites people to look at how science actually works and then reflect on how it can be part of a story that has meaning. It's not static because we're always discovering new things with science. And each time we discover something new, if we want to live generatively, we have to reorient ourselves to be more in tune with the new knowledge. Since we don't know everything,

Dwelling in mystery
and being open to uncertainty
is one of the great tasks
of a human being.

and the story is so big, a lot of different points of view can take place within it, space opens up for imagination regarding ways to do that, including fueling new questions for science to explore.

Sam: It sounds like science offers the foundation of the story, giving us factual knowledge, and that the humanities are employed to build on top of it with creativity and meaning.

Mary Evelyn: What we are really trying to do with *Journey of the Universe* is create a new genre of a fusion of science and humanities. We're not looking at science as just facts or numbers or equations or graphs, but science in relation to the humanities—literature, history, art, music, philosophy, and religion and so on. These are the disciplines that have tried to understand how humans have lived in the past and how might we live more integrally in the future. So *Journey* is a conscious fusion of fact, metaphor, and meaning. This can confuse people because they might think it's just about science. Other people might think it's only a spiritual vision. Actually it's a more subtle and complex coming together of various disciplines.

I would also like to point out that we're not trying to say that the *Journey of the Universe* perspective overrides longstanding cultural and religious systems that have given humans a sense of meaning, purpose, connection, and community. It is not a triumphal hegemonic science story. It's one that respects traditional stories but sees the unifying potential of this great epic of evolution.

Julianne: I have taught classes where, in between chapters of *Journey of the Universe*, we'd jump over and read some of Charles Darwin's work from the Galapagos. This pairing has helped students see how a scientist might be filled with a sense of wonder and how he was giving meaning to some of the things he was learning. Darwin himself was taking bits of evidence about the relationships between different beings and putting the flesh of meaning on it by saying, "We're kin with all of life and, as kin, we can have empathy for one another."

At the same time, though, some of this thinking was applied to eugenics with this idea of the survival of the fittest. Science by itself doesn't tell you what you should do with knowledge. You have to have other ways of knowing to blend with those observations in order for there to be meaning. We have been misusing science in order to misuse the earth. Now we have to pull ourselves back to contemplate new and fresh understandings combined with the desire to promote life.

Sam: This example highlights how, even though science does help provide a foundation of knowledge for us to interpret, there is still always so much we don't know. I wonder if you might speak about the relationship between mystery and meaning. What is your process for creating meaning out of facts that can be interpreted in various different ways?

Julianne: Let's start from the stars as an example. The ways that gravity and fusion, supernovas and atomic dust combine to bring forth Earth. I just can't stop thinking about it. There's a paradox of wanting more knowledge, but at the same time enjoying how much I don't know about it. In between the knowing and not knowing there is all this space for my imagination. The desire for simple answers is a way to try to control things. It doesn't work. Instead we can try to embrace and dwell in ambiguity.

Mary Evelyn: I love this notion of ambiguity along with a search for meaning. I think that's actually what creativity is. We don't know from where a poem arises or the composition of music. Beethoven was deaf and he was still composing music. There is an idea that creativity arises from sources beyond ourselves. If we're in tune with certain aspects of this living Earth system, we may pick up on something and then release a piece of art or music or whatever. But it's all very staggering. Some scientists at Princeton recently told us that we don't really understand how galaxies emerge, even though there's been a lot of science on it.

Dwelling in mystery and being open to uncertainty is one of the great tasks of a human being. Eventually we can "live the questions," as Rainer Maria Rilke said. *Meaning* is such a laden term, I hesitate even to use the word, but I do think that fundamentally we are meaning-making animals. We know that many other animals have communication and language and all kinds of creativity within their worlds, but the meaning dimension might distinguish us. And this kind of large-scale story opens us up to depths of meaning that we hadn't really thought about before.

This speaks to our capacity for symbolic consciousness, which is a dynamic change engine because we are all moved by symbols. You can see this is why the advertising and media worlds are so powerful. But if we can create the connectivity to these interrelated processes and then begin to reflect on them symbolically and reconfigure our own social, political, and economic patterning in relation to the patterning of nature, then we're releasing new kinds of energy for creativity.

Julianne: I agree. At least around me, people who are dealing with confronting the realities that we're faced with now sometimes don't want to talk about what's good about human beings. But we can rediscover that there are different ways to be human; there always have been. We don't have to be dominators; we don't have to have just simple answers. Even with climate change and the Anthropocene, there is still space to play together. Perhaps it's never been more important to do so.

Mary Evelyn: Yes, there is the simultaneous awareness in our time of the beauty of evolution and deep time and, at the same time, an awareness of extinction and this destruction we're causing on the planet. The whole process of evolution is threaded through with similar dynamics of loss and creativity. I think part of the joy that we're trying to evoke in *Journey* is that loss and creativity go closely together. They're intermingled and we can't avoid that. The suggestion is that in between these forces we may find our way forward as a species.   •

This interview was originally published on the Garrison Institute blog (https://www.garrisoninstitute.org) on July 20, 2016 and is used with permission.

Divine Patience

By Sam Shriver

Today's a good day for my ego to die; spirit live on in my heart, in my body, my mind.
               —"Wash It Away," Nahko and Medicine for the People

ABOUT A YEAR and a half ago, my life was "on track." I was an active, outgoing guy making the transition from undergrad into the professional world. I grew up on the East Coast, developed a thoroughly liberal political outlook, played college sports, had summer jobs abroad, and enjoyed being the middle of five children in a boisterous Catholic family. I had finished sixteen years of requisite schooling and was a year into my first job. I'll call this period Life Epoch One and, in June of 2015, it was about to end.

My friend Brian had come to visit me outside of Philadelphia, where I lived on my own. As we chatted over pints of Weihenstephan's delicious Hefeweissbier, we shared stories about the first year of post-grad life. He told heart-wrenching stories about working for the Jesuit Volunteer Corps with the Whiteclay and Assiniboine Tribes on the Fort Belknap Reservation in Montana. I mostly talked about the transition from school to full-time work, and how it wasn't that bad—just "increasingly vapid," I remember saying. I told him I was ready to move on to something new. We talked about relationships, or the lack thereof, and you might believe that we had matured slightly since school, because we began speculating about the possibility of finding love.

"I remember a professor who taught this German poet, Rilke," Brian recalled, "who completely redefined for me what it means to be in a relationship." This was the first time I had ever heard Rainer Maria Rilke's name. Brian went on to describe Rilke's view that the purpose of a relationship is for two individuals to protect one another's solitude. A compelling insight, to be sure, but I didn't go out in search of a girlfriend the next day. It was weeks before I thought of Rilke again. I asked my father if he had heard of the poet. He handed me Charlie Louth's translation of Rilke's *Letters to a Young Poet*. I've since read three different translations, but that first time through stopped me in my tracks.

Across time, space, and language, Rilke gave me permission to be patient. "The only advice I have is this: to go into yourself and to examine the depths from which your life springs," he writes in response to a young man's request for feedback on his poetry.[1] No matter how hard it is or how long it takes, according to Rilke, the answers must come from within. "*Everything* must be carried to term before it is born," he continued, reminding the young man that, in times of searching, "*patience* is all!"[2] Even as a poor, barely published twenty-seven-year-old (in the early twentieth century), Rilke struck just about every chord I have. A year after reading him, a year that consisted of many conversations, interior dialogue, and research, I feel I've just begun to understand the profundity of his message.

Patience comes from the Latin *patientia*, meaning "endurance" or "quality of suffering." The opposite, *impatientia*, literally means "weakness." In Chinese, another ancient and yet disparate language, patience is similarly defined as "enduring the heart" (耐心—*naixin*). From an etymological standpoint, it is clear that Rilke is unveiling actionable discernment language. Before being able to find a path that is wholly my own, I need to develop a capacity to endure the feelings that cause me uncertainty, insecurity, and fear—feelings that make me impatient. The ability to be patient with myself, in other words, is the ability to *be* myself.

This shook me. I never thought of patience as any more than a

Ask the big questions and let go of the need for answers.

lesson learned as a child, a rule my mother put between my twelve-year-old self and the next slice of cake. What I heard from Rilke was that I needed to look deeper. I knew I needed change, and my first impulse was to move.

In a matter of months, I went from sitting in a Philadelphia office to crying tears of joy in the middle of Edinburgh's Meadows Park—welcome to Life Epoch Two. If, as Søren Kierkegaard suggested, life is lived forward but understood backward, then I was leaping back without knowing it. But it didn't begin with understanding; I had to get really lost first, and then remain lost.

I left home with a backpack and spent three months traveling alone. With no itinerary to speak of, I figured I would go and see a lot of new places. In the end, I spent nearly the entire time wandering around Scotland. I fell in love with the wide-open parks of Edinburgh, the sprawling forests of the highlands, and the beautiful beaches on the Outer Hebrides. I was there in the dead of winter, so it was dark and cold, but that made stumbling upon Luskentyre Beach, with only the occasional furry highland cow for company, that much more beautiful. I ran around like I was the only human being on the planet. Then I lay down on the fine, white sand and looked out at the mountains, which appeared to be moving out into the ocean on either side, as if they knew of a better place.

I moved from town to town, reading and writing for hours each day. I felt at ease and yet truly motivated to digest new information. I found myself seeking out quiet places to read and record my thoughts on the road. After spending four years trying to stay away from the library at school—and never writing for pleasure, I snuck into Edinburgh University's library four times during my weeklong stay in the city. (All I had to do was lurk at the top of the narrow staircase, waiting for students to swipe their cards so I could follow them in.) I was eager for space to think.

So what happened to me? Why did I need permission from Rilke to open up and explore my life in the first place? I think there were two primary factors at play.

First, I didn't understand solitude. Maybe this was because my generation, on the whole, has been conditioned to be both impatient and averse to solitude. The potential for loneliness is a very intimidating idea for anyone, not to mention those of us who grew up immersed in a world of constant communication and immediate gratification. It's not our fault, but it is our responsibility.

In my childhood, I had been exposed to the world of saints and poets who often spent long periods of time, if not their entire lives, alone. But I never considered emulating them. Frankly, the often-solitary paths of people like St. Antony of Egypt and Emily Dickinson seemed like an archaic practice. My perspective changed during my time on the road.

While I didn't leap into any ascetic practices, simply spending time moving alone gave me a deep appreciation for the power of intentional retreat in the form of two important outcomes: perspective and confidence. The first came through separation from the world in which I was raised. This gave me the chance to see my life from a bird's-eye view. I could have anticipated a new sense of perspective, but I didn't realize that Rilke had also awoken me to a spiritual dimension. If being patient with myself was the path to discernment, then I truly had an internal compass. What's more, I now had the power to access it. I just needed to trust myself. Internalizing this understanding manifested as a wave of confidence. I felt overwhelmingly comfortable in my own skin.

This strength quickly turned into a newfound sense of responsibility for my role as a young man in society. This was the second factor, and revealed a clear dissonance: Patience and self-awareness aren't "manly." On the surface, this problem is nothing new. Men are conditioned to present a stoic, unchanging demeanor, antithetical to developing qualities that evoke compassion and empathy. I was less aware of how strongly this affected me as an individual. I was good at being an extrovert, but I wasn't paying nearly as much attention to my inner life. This had left me powerfully imbalanced. I had let myself become the one-dimensional "good guy," always happy to go along with the crowd.

When I sat down in Meadows Park, I felt as though my entire being had been liberated for the first time, and I experienced a flood of emotion—hence the tears. I started to look back and question the ways I had defined myself. I also realized that, as much as I had been affected by society, I was responsible for perpetuating unhealthy norms too. In this regard, I was beginning to notice the bifurcation of myself and society. I could see the times where I was operating from a sense of my own agency, versus the times where I was satisfying external norms that dictated who I thought I should be.

I spent a lot of time evaluating that overlap. It took a while to acknowledge that I was dealing with lifelong issues without concrete answers. Again, Rilke's mentorship provided a road map: "Love the questions themselves like locked rooms, like books written in a foreign tongue."[3] So that's what I tried to do: Ask the big questions and let go of the need for answers.

I BELIEVE THAT WILLINGNESS to sit with uncertain feelings is central to crossing the threshold from boyhood to manhood. MIT Senior Lecturer Otto Scharmer has shown that this is actually a measurable skill—our Spiritual Quotient (SQ). Most of us are familiar with IQ, or Intelligence Quotient, and possibly with EQ, or Emotional Quotient, which is assessed by measuring a range of emotional capabilities, including self-regulation and empathy. Scharmer suggests that SQ is an additional level of "intelligence," centered in the depths of our awareness and measured by our willingness to allow feelings to come and go. Someone with a high SQ, Scharmer explains, would be consistently operating at his or her threshold, where the ego yields to what she or he really wants to become.[4] In my experience, spiritual intelligence is as much a battle of willpower as it is a test of patience.

Rilke propelled me onto that threshold, where my past, present, and future collided, producing a beautiful transformation. My experience of letting go, opening up, and coming into my manhood revolved around trusting my solitude and redefining patience as a doorway into my soul. There are many things about the last year and a half that I can't put into words, but I have learned so much about life, and I'm eternally grateful for the time and space I have had to search. Brian and I catch up on occasion and, while our conversations retain a very familiar tone, each time we talk I'm reminded of how far we have both come since the conversation in that bar in Philadelphia.   •

Chrysalis

By Wm Paul Young

T HE IMAGINATION OF TRANSFORMATION is worlds removed from the arduous work of participating in real transformation. Ask any caterpillar. She spends her days largely focused on immediate self-gratification but, when seeing a butterfly pass by, is unexpectedly caught by the wonder of flight and beauty and an internal longing for...something. Even when the therapist aphid whispers to her, "You need to know that you are, by nature, a butterfly. That is the truth of who you are!" the caterpillar takes one look in the mirror, shakes her head, and looks for the nearest leaf to munch in consolation. She has no idea of the intense and excruciating journey that lies ahead of her, where, inside of suffering and what will seem to be death, there will emerge, not another being, but the truth of her being that has been there from the beginning.

It is true that we are not caterpillars. We are not as patient with timing, nor as methodical, nor attuned to the seasons and process. Like the caterpillar, however, we do spin and weave what will be our undoing, the cocoons of our façades, built to cover our shame or sense of not being enough, a shell that gives us a sense of identity but hides and inhibits the truth within. Of this truth, most of us live unaware.

Thankfully, time is a created thing and not a limitation to God. God has all the time in the cosmos. Each of us has a unique timetable, known only to the God who created us, and a unique process, because no two of us are the same. The depth and meticulous creativity that crafted you is accounted for by God. The weaving includes much of what you have never had any say about, let alone knew: the genetics of your parents, and their parents before them; the experience transmitted to you in the womb; the trauma of emergence into a world that might have been terrifying and antagonistic or kind and embracing; what your parents, or their absence, instilled in you; exposure to loss, or abuse in any form, or suffering—all of this causes us to begin to form a covering, something that hides the truth of who we are. The walls thicken with each experience and because of the ways we interpret such.

It took me thirty-eight years to build my chrysalis, the death chamber that was my façade, the thing that I thought was my best attempt at being me. Building this shell took everything I had and, even though it gave me a false sense of control and safety, I continued to grow within it until I no longer had any ability to move—or hardly even breathe. It was not only constricting; it was slowly killing me. It took a massive failure on my part to instigate taking the risk to believe that the chrysalis I had created was not me. I had placed all my hope in that shell, because I believed that the person who was trying to live inside of it was worthless—not good, but depraved. Better to present a shell that might win some sense of approval and affection than risk anyone finding out the truth of the disgusting person that has hidden inside.

The caterpillar suffers. In fact, if that creature is spared the tension, restriction, and arduous turmoil of emerging, it will not survive. We are not caterpillars. We want an extreme soul-makeover, a shortcut that saves us from suffering: "Please God, send me to Disney World and heal me by the time I get back." Even though we have read that "Everyone is salted with fire" (see Mark 9:49), we hate fire almost as much as we hate the idea of process.

What makes it even worse is that authentic personhood will only emerge inside community. We are created in the image and likeness of a God who has never been alone, and so "aloneness" has never existed within the being of God. We bring that darkness to the table, and paint the imagination of an alone God, because it is the projection of how we see ourselves.

During the blood-and-sweat work of my emerging as an authentic human being, certain characters in Scripture became significant in ways they had not been before. One of these was Jacob. He was born a twin and came out of the womb with one hand firmly gripping his brother's ankle. He was a usurper, a trickster, a controller, a manipulator, and a liar…and ultimately a progenitor of Jesus, the Messiah, God incarnate. Reading his story in the Hebrew Scriptures, it is not difficult to discern how Jacob's chrysalis was formed.

Decades later, his chrysalis has hardened into a fortress, a prison in which Jacob defined God, himself, and the universe—and yet, something within is alive. He wants to live. He is still desperate for the blessing of God.

Jacob has gathered everything that he owns, every way in which he has created his sense of identity—worth, value, significance, security, meaning, purpose, destiny, community, and love—into his chrysalis. He is traveling across the wilderness, surrounded by his cocoon, when he hears the news that his brother is approaching with a few hundred armed men (see Genesis 32). It is vital to remember that Jacob has been pursuing God his entire life, but that pursuit has been defined by his need to control. He wants to trust God, but he can't. He never could take that risk and now he believes that his comeuppance has arrived: judgment day. One more time, Jacob freaks and looks for a way out, a manipulation through which he can scramble and escape. He projects onto his brother all the faces of those throughout his life that he has defrauded and exploited—which includes this twin—and he is certain he is about to be killed.

I so identify with Jacob. The survival skills that we embrace as children become the very walls that inhibit our ability to grow and change. What kept us alive and safe prevents us from forming deep or lasting relationships and our habit is to resort to control rather than trust. Like Jacob, I grew up wanting approval and affection, the blessing of my father, but never thought I was worthy of it. Unlike Jacob's father, my dad was an abusive, angry disciplinarian who regularly communicated to me that I was fundamentally bad and a failure. But Jacob and I both believed the same lies: that we were not worthy of being loved and that, if we performed well enough, we could offset the truth of our depravity enough to win a blessing. So, like Jacob, I became a twister and a manipulator, a liar and a rascal, hidden inside a presentation of self-righteous intellectuality and theological superiority. We build our own prisons, constructed with the steel sinews of the webs of lies we believe.

Jacob now knows that he is a dead man walking—unless.... Out of desperation, does he commit the desperate act of trust? Not even close: He gathers up his wives, children, servants, and slaves, and sends them off in the direction of Esau and his armed soldiers. His hope is that Esau will either accept these as a gift that might appease his fury or get weary of killing before he reaches Jacob.

Those things we are willing to sacrifice to avoid our fears and protect the sanctity of our chrysalis can be directly correlated to our desperation and need to control. First, we often sacrifice our relationships, especially those closest to us. But that isn't enough. Jacob's fears overwhelm him like tides and, with each wave, he sends off more of his goods and possessions, including his animals, herdsman, and shepherds, and finally all his physical wealth, along with its overseers. He is willing to lose everything to save his own skin: his chrysalis.

Now he is alone—except for God, whom Jacob does not have the power to send away. God is patient. It has taken years to get to this place and God is unmoved. In one final act of desperation, Jacob takes on God, trying to get God to do his bidding. When we are overwhelmed by fear, we will wrestle with anyone and everyone, including God.

So they wrestle, God exerting only enough strength to not let Jacob win. Finally, after all these years, Jacob is finished, exhausted, out of resources, without an ability or option to control, and his deepest plea and longing rises to the surface. Wrestled from Jacob's lips is perhaps the first authentic prayer and plea he has ever uttered: "I am not going to let you go until you bless me."

God's immediate and surprising response is, "Tell me your name."

In January, 1994, my façade came crashing down, and I began an eleven-year process of extricating myself from my chrysalis. I was completely exposed and the deconstruction/reconstruction work was painful and arduous. I learned to live inside only a single day's grace, because more than one day was too much and too overwhelming. Early in this journey, I sat, reading this story of Jacob, and a light went on. "I've heard this before," I thought. "These words, I've heard them, not only in my own life, but in Jacob's. But where?"

Then it dawned on me. There is a scene at the beginning of Jacob's

The survival skills that we embrace as children become the very walls that inhibit our ability to grow and change.

life, where he manipulates his father's blessing and steals his brother's birthright as the firstborn son. It is Adam's family story all over again, a second-born son trying to acquire through iniquity the blessings of the firstborn—a blessing in which he was always included. Jacob enters a darkened room where his father lies sick. Jacob has even covered his body with the skin of animals to hide his deceit. He wants the blessing of his father: "I am not going to let you go until you bless me."

"What is your name?" his father asks.

"Esau," lies Jacob—and he gets, through treachery, what he thought would give him identity, value, worth, significance, security, meaning, purpose, destiny, community, and love.

"What is your name?" God asks, so many years later.

Finally, after years of groaning inside the chrysalis, the prison cracks apart and the door opens.

"Jacob," he admits. "The deceiver, the twister, the liar, the manipulator. That is who I am. That is all I am."

"It is not all you are, or who you truly are, but it is a start," is the response. "So, I am going to bless you and I am going to change your name to something that is true and real and right: Israel, the man who is conquered by God."

Oh, the day that love finally conquers us, changes us, gives us our true name!

There is a promise in the book of Revelation that is for anyone who is willing to work through the difficult and arduous process of the healing of the soul: "I will give him a white stone, and a new name written on the stone, which no one knows but he who receives it" (see Revelation 2:17).

God blessed Jacob—in that moment, throughout the rest of his life, and into eternity. Jacob limped for the rest of his life (the immediate blessing). He no longer could walk with a façade of perfection or control. His limp was obvious, as is mine. His relationships, including that with his brother, were restored and he learned to be a human being, alive and comfortable inside his own skin. This is also true in my life. And, generations later, through Jacob, was born the ultimate firstborn son, Jesus. It was his heel that Jacob had tried to grab, his blessing that Jacob had tried to manipulate for his own good and purpose—and, through the wrestling, Jacob discovered that it was in Jesus' love that he had always been included. •

Transforming Addiction

By Timothy King

I CAN'T REMEMBER MUCH about the day when everything went wrong. No obvious moment indicated that the standard outpatient procedure would lead to weeks in the ICU, months in the hospital, and almost a year out of work.

Memories of a dark hospital room and slowly blinking lights come back in fevered fits. Dislocated voices from intrusive floating faces were saying that things would be alright.

I had known pain before: crutches, casts, and stitches. But until this moment, pain had always been experienced as something outside of myself. Now it was all that was left of me.

The day turned into night turned into day turned into night. I had given up on crying for the pain to subside. My soul had turned to the guttural moan of Job: "Dear God, if this is my fate, may I never have been born at all."

I remember hearing the words "acute respiratory distress" and being moved to the ICU. I remember how my IV stand became a tree that blossomed with multi-colored ornaments hanging from stainless steel branches with cascading ripples of wires and tubes falling to my nose, arms, and chest.

Also hanging there was a clear plastic box containing a small bag marked hydromorphone—an opioid pain medication. The only moments when I remembered I was still a person and pain was an experience I was having—and not my entire existence—occurred every fifteen minutes when I pressed a small button that sent a pump whirring and boosted the normally slow trickle of the blessed, blessed, blessed analgesic already flowing.

Over the course of this medical odyssey, my 5' 10" frame dropped below 130 pounds, the whites of my eyes turned yellow, my stomach became distended, fevers spiked and dropped. There was vomiting, diarrhea, hallucinations, surgeries, procedures, and minutes that turned into hours that turned into days when the doctors would not allow me to place even a chip of ice in my mouth.

There were crying family members surrounding the hospital bed, desperate phone calls to find a specialist who could handle my case, and the moment when I heard the doctor say the words, "There is nothing more we can do."

It was after all of this, when I was home, stable, and recovering, that I learned I had developed a new complication. It was a disease related to some of the medication I had been, and was still, taking. Over two-and-a-half million people struggle with this disease in the United States annually. It is an illness that has reached epidemic proportions in our country, claiming the lives of seventy-eight people a day, with incidences of death quadrupling between 1999 and 2014, according to the Centers for Disease Control and Prevention.

The disease is opioid addiction.

My story of addiction is unremarkable. It was not the cause of my hospital stay but a result of it. I never doctor-hopped for pain meds or purchased them illegally. I never hit rock-bottom, pawned my mother's television set, or became a drug mule to pay for my habit. And, by God's grace, the disease was caught early.

During my journey of recovery, I came to understand more deeply than ever why addiction is called a disease. Some might think of an addict as a hard-living rock star who habituates their gluttony for an ever-higher high or an urban degenerate who feeds off the deepest depravities of human nature and becomes wealthy by destroying the lives of others. I discovered what many professionals have known for decades: Addicts aren't "bad" people, but those in the grip of something beyond their control.

WHAT AN OPIOID ADDICT LOOKS LIKE

AN OPIOID, FROM the root word opium, is a class of pain-relieving drugs that can vary in intensity from fentanyl (extreme) to codeine (mild). According to the Department of Health and Human Services, more than 240 million prescriptions were written for legal opioids in 2014—more than enough for every adult in the United States to have their own bottle. From 1999 to 2014, the period in which opioid overdose deaths quadrupled, so too did the sales of prescription opioids.

The widespread nature of the opioid epidemic—that reaches across typical class, race, and geographical stereotypes—has challenged myths of who drug addicts are. It has also widened the lens, revealing more moral actors participating in the crisis, beyond the addict. Years of distorted public policy; overworked and undertrained doctors; intentionally misleading pharmaceutical marketing; and even watered-down theology that reduces people to disembodied moral agents instead of whole human persons, created in the image and likeness of a good God; have all contributed, through sins of both omission and commission.

Many opioid addicts began using these drugs for legitimate physical ailments, merely following their doctors' orders. In fact, the American Society of Addiction Medicine reports that four out of five heroin addicts started with prescription opioid medications, with nearly all reporting that they eventually switched to heroin because of the price.

Our mental picture of an addict should include the high-school honors student who breaks her arm skateboarding and is prescribed an opioid by her doctor.

Or the middle-aged factory worker who has permanent back pain from his job and is prescribed an opioid by his overworked doctor, who misses the fact that his patient is severely depressed.

Or, think of me: A white, college-educated, employed, middle-class Christian from a good family who grew up on a farm in New Hampshire.

My complex medical history was the genesis of my addiction. In 2009, I suffered from acute necrotizing pancreatitis caused by a procedure commonly known as an ERCP. I was sent home with a PICC line, a sort of semi-permanent IV, in my arm. The IV connected me to a pump to receive most of my liquid and almost all of my nutrition for twelve hours a day. As I was able, I was supposed to slowly introduce into my diet clear liquids, then broths, then other easily digestible food.

Progress was slower than expected. I continued to experience pain with too much liquid. When I introduced light food, the pain would increase and I'd start vomiting.

During a follow-up with my doctor, he determined that the cause of my ongoing pain and inability to eat was gastroparesis. The pain medicine I had been taking was deadening the nerve endings in my digestive tract and hindering my ability to process food. In other words, the pain medicine was now causing the pain. The more I took to relieve the pain, the more pain I felt.

That's when the doctor told me: "Tim, you need to know you are addicted to pain medicine."

I felt my stomach drop and defenses rise as he said these words. All the stereotypes of addicts I didn't think I held crept into my mind. Because I was legitimately in pain, I thought I couldn't be an addict.

The doctor continued, "That isn't a judgment on you. I'm not saying you've done anything wrong or that you aren't still in pain. But we've been giving you this pain medicine for so long, your body is now dependent on it. It has gone from helping you to hurting you."

I relaxed. I let my defenses down and loosened my grip on my justifications.

The widespread nature of the opioid epidemic—that reaches across typical class, race, and geographical stereotypes—has challenged myths of who drug addicts are.

"I'm not going to just take the pain medicine away from you when you need it," the doctor said. "But if I make that commitment to you, I want you to make a commitment to me. Will you take less whenever you can? For a while, you couldn't have made it without the pain medicine. Now, to fully heal, you need to eventually stop taking it."

I took a deep breath of relief. I wasn't "bad." I hadn't done anything "wrong." I had a new disease, a complication from my medication, and I had a doctor who was there and ready to help.

THE BODY AND THE WILL

In July, 2016, Congress passed legislation to address the opioid crisis and heroin epidemic. Even using the language of "crisis" and "epidemic" to describe the bill indicates a shift in mentality. The legislation acknowledges a growing medical consensus that the addict is subject to a disease—one with deep biological and psychological roots that often preclude individual choice.

This landmark legislation marked an important (albeit incomplete) step forward in reorienting public policy to reflect this new consensus. Framing addiction as chronic disease does not remove the moral choices involved but gives us a broader framework for understanding them. We can't ignore the reality of our bodies and, when it comes to opioid addiction (and other addictions), part of the effect of those chemicals is to rewire the brain, making it more difficult or nearly impossible to change patterns of thought and behavior.

One commonly used analogy helping us understand addiction is heart disease. Like all analogies, it doesn't explain everything, but it has the virtue of pointing out how clogged arteries cannot be cleared up by giving a pep talk to the patient or telling him to stop breathing so hard after climbing a set of stairs. Its causes are found in a mix of hereditary, environmental, and lifestyle choices.

It's also helpful to think about how often our physical state and surroundings influence our actions. Have you ever had to apologize for something you said before you had your cup of coffee, or maybe feelings of anger and impatience that you later realized were mostly resolved by eating a sandwich?

But the sense that addiction is solely a moral problem is hard to eradicate. After I clearly understood my addiction as a disease, I still battled internally with my self-image. I grew up with the "Just Say No" campaigns aimed at warning youth about illegal drugs. In that model, those with moral fortitude say "no," and moral degenerates say "yes." Those who said "no" received praise, and those who said "yes" were shamed and punished.

IT TAKES A VILLAGE OF GRACE

I REMOVED THE FENTANYL patch first and switched to taking only Dilaudid. Within a day I could again feel my body in ways I did not realize I had been missing. At the same time, it felt as if a thick, protective comforter had been ripped off from around me while I lay shivering and naked on my bed. Pain that had been blunted refocused and pressed out from the inside.

The doctor was right; I could handle the pain now without the same levels of opioids. But I couldn't have continued my recovery if it were all up to the strength of my will alone.

My mother, a nurse, had been with me at that crucial doctor's appointment. What would have happened if she had reacted with judgment instead of support? My employer at the time, Sojourners, had gone far above and beyond, not just legal requirements, but any general expectations to ensure I was financially secure, had access to quality health care, and had the hope of a job to return to. A friend who was starting a church in his living room picked me up on Sunday mornings. I was still taking pain pills to get through the service, but I stayed connected to a community defined by openness, honesty, mutual vulnerability, grace, and love.

So much more powerful than saying "no" to an opioid was the opportunity to say "yes" to a slow return to a life of flourishing.

As my body recovered and the pain subsided, I talked with my doctor and we stepped down from four-milligram to two-milligram pills. I began yoga and light exercise. Each step felt like a choice that rubbed against the grain of my body and mind.

I remember looking at a near-empty bottle of pain pills and feeling nervous and insecure. I had switched to primarily over-the-counter pain relievers and one strong pain pill a day. When my doctor told me I could still get another refill if I needed it, I said no. I had determined that would be my last.

It was not an easy goodbye. The feeling was like the tremor in your hand when your blood sugar drops. Desire spreads out to every cell of your body, as if each one is making its own demand, aching and promising to be satisfied with just a little more.

These feelings of withdrawal and the troubled sleep that came with them were intense for the first few days. Months later, they would flare up again as a reminder of what had been—and the perilously thin line between me and the mounting numbers of long-term addicts and overdose victims.

I had to make the choice to recover from my addiction, but I could not have recovered without the choices of others. Many addicts also experience the reality that they would not have become addicts without their own choices, but they also would not have become addicts if not for the choices of others.

ADDICTS R US

WHEN I READ story after story of tragic overdoses and the harm addiction can bring to communities and families, I no longer see the separation I once did. I see now that my story of addiction is not so far from that of a white addict living in rural West Virginia or a black addict on the streets of Chicago. The origins of our use and the names of the substances might change, but our stories are fundamentally the same. Most addicts are addicts because their substance of choice really does do something for the pain they experience, whether that pain is physical, emotional, spiritual, or a mix of all three.

What I didn't realize I needed to hear, and which my doctor affirmed, was that I was still a "good" person—and I had an addiction. In a sense, I had not chosen to become an addict. Addiction had chosen me.

In struggling with my own sin, I have too often obsessed over Genesis 3 (the Fall) and functionally forgotten Genesis 1 and 2, which affirm that we are created good. And, as Augustine, among others, has reminded us, while we might be born into sin, there is no power great enough to take away the fact that we have been made in the divine image.

I've realized that the word "addict" is a particularly useful descriptor for who I have always been. I always resonated with Paul's lament:

All who acknowledge their own shortcomings and realize that they cannot eliminate them through their own power have admitted that they too are addicts.

"I do not do the good I want to do, but the evil I do not want to do—this I keep on doing" (see Romans 7:19).

Some who have never experienced the furious grip of chemical dependence are tempted to split the world into "addicts" and "non-addicts," morally bad and morally good. As I've said, I did not realize how fully I had embraced this view until faced with my own opioid addiction. Now, I realize that the world is divided between addicts who have begun to face their addictions and those who live under the illusion that they have none.

All who have come to the point where they acknowledge their own shortcomings and realize that they cannot eliminate them through their own power have admitted that they too, in their own way, are addicts. The addiction might be to food, shopping, status symbols, the need to be "right," the need to be needed, or the need to feel moral superiority over those who struggle with less "societally acceptable" sins.

One of the most powerful teachings the church can embrace in light of this crisis is to say, "Let the one who is not an addict cast the first stone."

While addiction science has made strides, there is still no silver bullet. Already there are stories of innovative addicts who have found new ways to abuse the medications intended to help them. Any approach that reduces addiction to a problem of brain chemistry and fails to acknowledge humans as moral actors will ultimately fail. But leading researchers, and those discussing public initiatives, have gone a long way to acknowledge the importance of a both/and methodology.

Churches can be cultural epicenters for shifts in societal norms. Our communities are built by and for wounded healers who recognize that no one is entirely free of addiction. It is in this weakness of each of us, and of the church as a whole, that Christ's strength is made perfect.

The longer that addiction is seen as a struggle for the "sinners out there" and not at the heart of the struggle of each and every one of us, the longer this problem will make headlines and remain in the shadows. Sin takes its deepest root in the cover of darkness, where it is never given a name. When our affliction is named for what it is and brought into the light, that's when darkness may be overcome. •

The original version of this article, "Just Say No to Shame," first appeared in the December 2016 issue of Christianity Today. *Used by permission of Christianity Today, Carol Stream, Illinois 60188.*

The Exhilarations
of Lymphoma:
A Year in the Life

By Christopher Spatz

AFTER FIFTY-TWO YEARS of remarkable, fortunate good health, I can't say I ever anticipated finding myself in an oncologist's office, being told, "The one certainty is that, without treatment, you have a terminal disease." Aside from a tonsillectomy when I was five, I had never been hospitalized. I had never broken a bone, never had my wisdom teeth removed. I had never suffered with more than childhood asthma, seasonal allergies, and the occasional migraine, never mind facing an existential threat.

In January, I noticed a bulge in front of my right ear, near where my jaw is hinged. Initially I thought it was a strain because it was not noticeably sore. Fairly quickly, over a matter of weeks, the swelling spread along my jawline. I began to feel it inside my mouth, under my gums. I developed a firm lump on the right side of my chin, and another below my jaw that showed in my neck. I saw my doctor in

January and February. He was certain that I had an impacted salivary gland and said it wasn't uncommon for the entire area to be as involved as it was. I made sure he felt the various bumps and saw the discoloration and inflammation of my gums on the right side. He was insistent on his diagnosis and said he would see me again in three months if it hadn't cleared up on its own. So I went on with life.

As June approached, although I still wasn't in pain, the condition had not abated; in fact, I was starting to worry about the effects inside my mouth and on my teeth. I had gradually noticed my speech being affected and became self-conscious. I arranged an appointment with the physician assistant. She carefully examined the swollen areas and consulted with the doctor. She assured me that he was still certain of his original diagnosis, but stated that I should have a CT scan of my head and neck to pinpoint the source of the problem and determine the necessary treatment. I remember thinking that I hoped it would be a simple procedure so I could get on with life.

Two days after the scan, the physician assistant called to tell me that several abnormal masses were noted and that the next step was a tissue biopsy. Although I was advised not to worry, I was aware that she had pulled strings to get the biopsy done right away. The procedure took place before a long weekend, and several days passed before my phone rang. The surgeon cheerfully let me know that I had been diagnosed with "diffuse large B-cell non-Hodgkin lymphoma"—an aggressive form of cancer—and I was being referred to an oncologist to determine options.

When I shared what I had just learned with my partner, Larry, it was a catastrophic moment for me—the time I felt closest to panic. Among my initial reactions were anger with my doctor for standing firm while I lived with cancer for six months and terror about how far this aggressive disease could have spread during that time.

From the start, Larry maintained a calming presence, determined to look forward and not to despair. We learned much from the oncologist and from our own research. Though distressing, we learned that this form of cancer has a successful treatment rate. Knowing this allowed me to confront it with less dread. There would be decisions to make; multiple treatment options fell within accepted practice. First, the stage of progression would be determined through a full PET/CT scan and a bone marrow biopsy. Both of these unfamiliar procedures caused a considerable sense of foreboding. However, these proved to

The time had come to put away my old inner dialogues and refuse to allow new stories to keep growing out of old wounds.

be the first of many opportunities to breathe deeply and participate fully and bravely. I experienced my first exhilaration when we learned that the cancer hadn't spread beyond my jaw and neck.

I never believed that God had bestowed this disease on me, nor did I believe it would be taken away because I asked. The prayers I offered were for courage, strength, tolerance, a fighting spirit, and confidence in making the best decisions. I refused to be fearful or to despair. Rather, I made the choice to live one day at a time and to expect to be part of the future. I was open to and cognizant of loving and being loved, and aware of the care and compassion extended to me from many sources. I was humbled by sincere expressions of support from coworkers, acquaintances on social media, and friends and family. I learned that I was placed on many people's prayer lists, most of whom I didn't know, thanks to my dear mother. I was thankful for feeling genuinely cared for by the doctors, nurses, technicians, and other medical staff. And, of course, I was constantly encircled at home by the abundant love of Larry and our three very devoted Great Danes: Bentley, Lexi, and Declan.

In mid-July I began chemotherapy treatments. I was apprehensive about being completely depleted and debilitated by chemo, but physically and emotionally I endured it very well. Infusion was an all-day affair, requiring extraordinary patience on my part. I sat, attached to an IV tube, while bag after bag of fluid dripped ever so slowly into my veins. I snacked and napped while Larry sat with me the entire time. The most disquieting delivery was the chemical that would cause tissue damage if it leaked, requiring the administering nurse to completely suit up and don two sets of gloves for her own protection.

My second exhilaration came only two days after the very first round of treatment, when the tumors I'd been living with for months were, suddenly, almost undetectable to the touch. It was quickly evident that the combination of chemicals was finding its targets and doing its job.

I felt some guilt at the overall ease with which I tolerated chemo. I had very little nausea and retained a healthy appetite. With the exception of each treatment day and the day following, I continued working through challenging fatigue. I was determined to power through, however badly I felt. I was grateful that the daily structure and routine kept me from worry and self-pity. Larry provided me with a nutritious diet and helped find foods that appealed to me while avoiding spicy foods that irritated my digestive system. Our weekend outings with the dogs, while strenuous, presented invigorating moments for understanding gratitude.

I was subjected to three infusions, each three weeks apart. Blood panels and check-ins with the oncologist followed every cycle. At the same time, I was managing a varying regimen of pills. With the concluding PET/CT scan, I experienced my third exhilaration—no trace of the tumors was visible and the lymphoma was declared to be in complete remission.

DURING THE TWO to three years prior to that July, I had been challenged with a snowballing feeling of profound change, uncertainty, and lack of clarity in my life. Much of it emanated from my vocation, but transcended into deeper questions about who I was and where I wanted to be.

In the days before I was diagnosed with lymphoma, I had felt myself approaching a critical juncture, questioning my longevity and ability to keep going. I had persistent bouts of anxiety and helplessness; sleeplessness kept me worn down and dragging. I think I had a deep, nagging, pervasive sense that something serious was about to happen because my jaw was not healing. Essentially, something needed to shift—and abruptly, dramatically, everything did: "The one certainty is that, without treatment, you have a terminal disease."

After the diagnosis and during the new treatment rituals, life was remarkably more straightforward. I felt like I'd been saved from wallowing in my doldrums and discouragement. I felt liberated from philosophical concerns around life and livelihood. The focus of my energy for the next several months was on getting well, managing treatment, and taking care of myself. I settled into a new pattern, with a new, clear set of priorities, and I enjoyed it. One of my late father's favorite expressions, "The main thing is not to get excited," touched me constantly. I felt a peace that allowed me to really live in the present moment, freed from day-to-day worries, and to forgive the many inconveniences in my life and livelihood—most of which seemed insignificant now. I was able to be patient with the treatment steps, with my limitations, with managing side effects, and with the speed of my recovery.

That remission announcement was not, however, the end of the story. Up next: Time to plan decisions about further treatment. Accepted practices provided two options: (1) I could continue with three additional infusions for a total of six or (2) I could discontinue chemotherapy and begin localized radiation treatments. Both protocols were expected to be equally effective and produce the same long-term prognosis. I met with a radiation oncologist to discuss the details so that I could carefully weigh the benefits and risks of both chemo and radiation. Because I felt the tingling beginnings of neuropathy in my fingertips and toes—a common side effect of chemo that can be cumulative and permanent—I chose to switch to radiation.

I underwent seventeen treatments—far less than for other types of cancer. Each treatment involved being "snapped" down to a table with my face positioned under a snugly molded plastic mask that immobilized my head and shoulders. The technicians would run the computerized cycle from the safety of a control booth, separated from me by a massive vault door. The machinery surrounded me, laser aligned, whirring and flashing and creating the sensation of ozone in my sinuses. Each treatment took about ten minutes, after which I'd head out to work for the day.

As if to test me further, the worst suffering followed my elation of being in remission. During the second week of radiation treatments, I developed lesions in my mouth—inside my cheek, along the edge of my tongue, and in the back of my throat—that made eating, swallowing, and talking arduous and painful. I felt my own flesh was turning against me. I was unable to chew anything and became incredibly sensitive to hot and cold temperatures and anything spicy. During chemotherapy I had already been forced to give up my beloved New Mexican cuisine with its characteristic red and green chiles, but now I couldn't be certain what type of seasoning would cause searing agony.

Larry mastered mild vegetable soups that could be blended so I could manage them. I used an anesthetizing mouth rinse and applied lidocaine to the affected areas so I could eat and sleep. My sense of taste diminished and food seemed overly bland, sometimes flavorless.

The greatest impact on our relationship—and the only time Larry and I ever exploded at each other during this ordeal—happened over our frustration with his attempts to keep me fed and strong and my inability to partake of, much less enjoy, the food he worked so hard to prepare. At one point, even eating Jell-O was insurmountable. I knew that Larry was anguished by taking me to daily radiation appointments because he felt the hurt and helplessness of living with what those daily treatments were doing to me. The side effects worsened each day, and we anxiously counted the days until treatments were over. Furthermore, these side effects did not begin to subside until more than three weeks after my final treatment, and continued to flare up from time to time for many more months. During this time, Larry and I grew in our mindfulness and practiced compassion toward one another.

FINALLY, MY FOURTH exhilaration occurred the day in late October when I rang the brass bell in the treatment room three times and recited the exit poem aloud, announcing my release from treatment. Larry and I shed tears of deep gratitude.

But very soon, and unanticipated, my old disgruntlements awakened from dormancy, like an enormous pendulum swinging back from the top of its arc. The end of treatment created a void and my erstwhile resentments and irritations came streaming back in. I lost the tolerance that had seemed nearly effortless during treatment. The gratification and calm that had buoyed me during the past difficult months suddenly departed. I blew up, I behaved badly, and I had to make some apologies.

It was then that I was walloped by the realization that my treatment period offered a tangible model of what still could be. I could feel what was absent in the emptiness and longed to bring it back. I had been the recipient of compassion exemplified and wanted to share that outwardly. Perhaps I couldn't change my situations, but I had the power to change my perceptions of them—to let go and focus on calmness, fulfillment, and acceptance. The time had come to put away my old inner dialogues and refuse to allow new stories to keep growing out of old wounds.

Perhaps the end of this phase of the tale isn't so much another exhilaration as it is a willing surrender and hopeful anticipation. The oncologist reported that we could be eighty-five to ninety percent assured that the lymphoma would not return and that we had achieved a complete cure. For once, I truly observed the arrival of the New Year as a milestone. •

The Well

Be thankful now for having arrived,
for the sense of having drunk from a well,
for remembering the long drought
that preceded your arrival and the years
walking in a desert landscape of surfaces
looking for a spring hidden from you for so long
that even wanting to find it now had gone
from your mind until you only remembered
the hard pilgrimage that brought you here,
the thirst that caught in your throat;
the taste of a world just-missed
and the dry throat that came from a love
you remembered but had never fully wanted
for yourself, until finally after years making
the long trek to get here it was as if your whole
achievement had become nothing but thirst itself.

But the miracle had come simply
from allowing yourself to know
that you had found it, that this time
someone walking out into the clear air
from far inside you had decided not to walk
past it anymore; the miracle had come
at the roadside in the kneeling to drink
and the prayer you said, and the tears you shed
and the memory you held and the realization
that in this silence you no longer had to keep
your eyes and ears averted from the place
that could save you, that you had been given
the strength to let go of the thirsty dust laden
pilgrim-self that brought you here, walking
with her bent back, her bowed head
and her careful explanations.

No, the miracle had already happened
when you stood up, shook off the dust
and walked along the road from the well,
out of the desert toward the mountain,
as if already home again, as if you deserved
what you loved all along, as if just
remembering the taste of that clear cool
spring could lift up your face and set you free.

—David Whyte[1]

Repairing My Inner Two States

By Tiffany Keesey

A FEW MONTHS AGO, I traveled throughout Israel with a group of social activists in a collective exploration of how to address the world's most pressing challenges. As we journeyed, it became clear that we were in a country grappling with its identity, dealing with deep-rooted paradoxes and multidimensional challenges. This is an innovative, start-up nation that celebrates both its antiquity and its modernity. It is a "holy land" filled with internal tensions, surrounded by enemies on all sides—a land of refuge for those seeking safety and yet also an occupying state. Israelis seem to be able to embrace paradox without reservation. "The only way forward is a two-state solution," they tell us, "but Israel will not survive a two-state solution."

As we struggle to hold all the paradoxes in a dynamic tension, I become increasingly aware of the unresolved paradoxes within myself. There is me, a thirty-something social entrepreneur in a group of like-minded peers, who is leading morning yoga and engaging in discus-

I could not grasp at the time that my small notion of God had to die in order to make room for a more expansive understanding of Divine Reality.

sions of our collective commitment to *tikkun olam*, repairing the world. This version of myself, the one with which I identify the most, believes that vulnerability is the birthplace of connection and that transformed people transform the world. She holds the words of poets and mystics as her sacred texts and doesn't know what to do with religious labels.

Following me in this journey through the cobbled streets of Jerusalem, under the desert skies of Ein Gedi, and throughout the vibrant markets of Tel Aviv, is a shadow version of my younger self. This slightly awkward, beautifully naïve teenager would have been on a very different trip. It would be a youth group trip, most likely, organized through her evangelical church. There would have been lots of singing worship songs, referencing bible verses, and looking for opportunities to tell strangers about Jesus. She would have written off anything that would have challenged her worldview, because she knew deep down that she had the truth. She would be happy in a way that I partially envy now, because it all was so simple. God was in control.

I have tried very hard to distance myself from this younger self. I cringe over the Christian clichés she used, the apologetics classes she took to prepare for mission trips, and the way she dutifully upheld purity codes because she believed that all authority existed outside herself. Looking back, I feel ashamed that she tried to convert her friends because, without knowing it, she was communicating that they were somehow less-than. I wish she would have pushed back on the teachings just a little bit and found her voice in small acts of rebellion. I wish she could have seen past what she was taught to focus on, which blinded her to the real systems of oppression and evil in the world.

As we enter Jerusalem and prepare for Shabbat, it dawns on me that I have very intentionally, albeit unconsciously, created and reinforced the distance between us. I have rejected her beliefs, criticized her religion, and tried to forget. But, mostly, I have judged her and shamed her. I am only now realizing that this kind of self-shame is a type of violence.

Perhaps, in shaming her, I was trying to prevent the inevitable pain and trauma that followed. As I was exposed to the reality of human suffering in other parts of the world, my religious scaffolding began to fall apart. I found mainstream theology to be too rigid, too narrow, and too exclusively divided across race, class, gender, and sexual-orientation lines. I watched the church overlook real suffering while fighting its culture wars, and the dissonance between my internal values and my religious upbringing became too disparate to ignore. In the unraveling, I felt abandoned by the God that I knew and loved.

I could not grasp at the time that my small notion of God had to die in order to make room for a more expansive understanding of Divine Reality. I could not foresee that, in the confusion, I would go inward and trust my inner wisdom for the first time. I certainly did not see that it was necessary—all of it—and that every loss was a part of the continual unfolding that was leading to greater expansion. At the time, I just experienced the pain of it all.

I find myself wishing that I could have bypassed the pain; that I could somehow birth a new identity without having to go through the labor. And yet, here I am, in the place where Jesus was killed, buried, and resurrected. Here, I'm forced to confront my relationship with my former self and, by extension, her Christianity. I no longer believe that God needed a sacrifice to bridge a fundamental chasm with humanity. No, that was never the problem to begin with. I now believe that Jesus was revealing the fundamental pattern of things—the ongoing process of death and rebirth. In order to move from constriction to expansion, there must be a death to the egoic self. Loss and suffering clear away what no longer serves us, making space for something new.

As our group approaches the Western Wall, there is an energy that surrounds us and invites us to participate in this sacred space. We can sense the beauty and brokenness of humanity in the hope and prayers of those who have come before. Perhaps that is why I decide, this time, to invite my young self into this space with me. I decide to embrace her fully for who she is. Here, she softens and I start to remember how scary and tumultuous her world was. There was the teenage pain of needing to belong, the overwhelming fear of almost losing her mom to cancer, the pressure to conform and perform. I remember how much she needed to believe in something deeper, something greater sustaining her. How could she have done it any differently? How could I possibly have anything but compassion for her?

Brené Brown states that shame cannot survive when empathy is present, and in this tiny, radical act of love, my shame folds under the weight of compassion for who I once was. Compassion, in turn, gives way to a grief that has been there all along, waiting to be felt.

As I press my palms to the wall, the ancient limestone seems to welcome it all, just as it has welcomed the grief and hopes and prayers of all who have come before. In this place, I am unbelievably grateful for it all. I am grateful for the structure and also for the unraveling; for a process that has led me to a deepening trust in the unfolding. As Lady Julian of Norwich said, "First there is the fall, and then the recovery from the fall, and both are the mercy of God."[1] If I had to do it all over again, I would choose my life—shadow and all. It has brought me here. •

A Surrender to Love

By Paula D'Arcy

Mystics and sages of all traditions speak of the inner fire, the divine spark hidden in our very cells and in all that lives. This flame of love is the pure presence of God. Because of it, life is sustained. No power is greater. If the heart surrenders to this force of love, a true shift in the way you see may come to be.

IT IS A WARM afternoon in May and I am with thirty-five female inmates at the county jail near my home in Texas. Also seated in the facility's worn classroom are jail guards and staff, two singers, and a pianist. Whatever we are able to offer by being here, we have one hour in which to do it. The plan is for the singers to open with a rich musical program. I'll follow their performance using some of the song lyrics as a basis for writing exercises and points of discussion. We want to help the women experience something beyond the realities of low self-esteem, shame, and failure that are too often reinforced by the prison system.

In preparation for today, I've been in conversation with the singers for several weeks. Both Laura and Sarajane are members of a Grammy Award-winning professional choir known as Conspirare. The size of the choir fluctuates, depending upon the demands of the repertoire during the concert season, but the Conspirare singers generally number a hundred voices. So we are a skeletal crew today, but the talent of these two women, a soprano and mezzo-soprano, is exceptional.

As soon as the singers selected the music they wanted to offer today, they sent me copies of the lyrics. Their choices were well-suited to the dialogue I hoped to inspire. They had taken great care to offer a wide variety—everything from pop music and Broadway musicals to more traditional pieces. The selections were about hope and healing. I only had one misgiving. The singers had also included a piece from the French opera *Lakmé*, by Léo Delibes, called "Flower Duet." I wondered whether opera would have a wide enough appeal and was concerned that, since the lyrics would be in French, their meaning would be lost. I wrestled for several days with whether or not to say something about my reservation. I am forever grateful that I decided to remain silent and trust what they had chosen. Little did I know or guess what we were all about to experience.

The singers decided to open the program with the duet from the opera. As the inmates arrived and found seats, there was a lot of restless energy in the room—heads turned each time someone new came in, and there were multiple greetings and a steady hum of whispered conversations. In addition to that background noise, there was the ongoing interruption of loudspeaker announcements, plus the voices of those walking down the corridor past our door. Guards also walked back and forth inside the room, monitoring the rows. At some point, I gave up hope that we would be able to create a quiet atmosphere. At 1:00 p.m., Laura and Sarajane welcomed everyone and begin to sing the first notes of "Flower Duet."

When we are finally willing to meet "what is" and stop insisting on our own version of life, real change and transformation become possible.

In the same way that Rilke writes about the darkness being able to pull in everything, "shapes and fires, animals and myself"[1]—in exactly that way—the sheer beauty of the singers' voices and the magnificence of the opera changed the room. It became completely still and we were somehow inside the song. The music pulled us into the brevity of a lifetime; the mistakes we make; our longings for things to be different, to be better; the despair of being without hope; and the pure and the holy. When I turned around to look, I saw that many inmates were overcome by emotion. Something sublime was moving in that room—a sound that directly entered our hearts.

I forgot about time and our schedule and anything else that had seemed important just minutes before. The jail was taken over by the ascending beauty of the music. A powerful force moved in that plain and simple classroom, pressing its way through the life circumstances represented by the women seated in the rows of metal chairs. It was as if the enveloping sound was saying to a hidden place in each of us: *Something great is alive in you, and something more than this surface reality is intended for your life. Beyond your circumstances lies a different destiny.*

It was not just the inmates who were visibly affected, but everyone else who was present as well. Something inexpressible in the music had broken our hearts open, and the experience could not have been planned or commanded into being. There was no strategy, just the unmistakable movement of Spirit. I felt a growing awareness that it was important not to go back into hiding, but to remain within the openness that was being granted.

I T WASN'T THE FIRST time I had felt this. In the early 1980s, when I was still trying to put the pieces of my life together after the sudden deaths of my husband and daughter in a drunken-driving accident, I felt challenged by everything. In the blink of an eye my conclusions, my worldview, and my image of God were upended. It was an unsettling time. I kept reaching to the mind, searching for ideas and philosophies to guide me. That old way of managing things was very familiar.

But the mind could not bring me where I needed to go. It was a long while before I turned in a different direction and began to look within. Eventually I saw that the seeds of a greater journey are waiting in everything and I understood that, when the time is right—when we are finally willing to meet "what is" and stop insisting on our own version of life—real change and transformation become possible.

It was an important waking-up. My familiar default was to rely on old voices and experiences—on the mind's many concepts and ideas. Yet the force of love that sustains life is not a concept, and there are not a set of holy conditions to attain. As I opened my heart, love moved through the pain and slowly changed my sight. Things that once seemed fixed and defining were unmasked. When the "Flower Duet" was sung in the jail, it was again an experience of the flame of love—the brilliance of God that poet Robert Browning calls "the imprisoned splendor."[2] Pulled in by that love, even the reality of serving time in jail could be temporarily forgotten. The music's power momentarily lifted us beyond that room.

There is a well-known scene in the film, *The Shawshank Redemption*, when a selection from the opera *The Marriage of Figaro* is played over the prison loudspeaker system, and the prison population is suddenly transported. In the same way, love was present to us that afternoon—not as something inspiring, but as a living reality.

When the end of our sixty minutes was near, I held up a small plastic globe and asked the women to pass it around. "When you receive the globe," I said, "hold it for a moment and imagine that the heart of the world is actually in your hands, and that the openness of your heart affects it." They might have rejected this request as a silly exercise, but they didn't. I watched as the globe moved across the rows. Some closed their eyes as they held the world, and many held it up to their hearts. Then a bell rang abruptly and our time was up. The inmates filed out of the room and we began to tidy the classroom and stack chairs. There was no visible sign of our experience other than what still moved within us.

It was then that I noticed some writing on a piece of paper left on one of the seats. I picked it up. As part of a writing exercise, I had asked the inmates to respond to the question: "What do you want others to know about you that they don't see?" One inmate's response was written on the paper I'd just found:

I want you to know that I am stronger than anyone could imagine, and I am now allowing myself the opportunity to live.... I want you to know that I'm living into my passion with clarity.... I want you to know that I'm now living a life that is authentic.

I held her words in my hands, just as the globe had been held. In advance of our coming, when I'd been asked to submit a brief description of how this day would unfold, I never guessed that someone would write the words I was now reading. We had been offered an invitation much greater than I could have foreseen.

The voices of the inmates and the inspiration they felt were real. Our hearts had been directly impacted by the power alive in the music, and that brush of love called us to something infinitely more. God came to us disguised as a county jail—God came to us disguised as our lives, and that is always true. Life is the place where the inner fire can be met.

FAMED PSYCHIATRIST and concentration camp survivor, Viktor Frankl, was once interviewed by a group of colleagues. They were eager to learn how to inspire in their own clients the resilience and transformation shown by some survivors of the camps, men and women who rose above that terrifying experience. Frankl told them that there was no method, no means to bring this about—it comes from within. Seeds of transformation blossom when the heart's surrender to love is complete and sincere.

In October, I drove to Alabama with two friends to meet a man named Tom Hendrix, who lives in a small, wooded haven in the northwest part of the state. My friends wanted me to experience a wall Tom had built in memory of his great-great-grandmother, a member of the Yuchi tribe. In the late 1830s, she took the long walk that many tribes were forced to take in accordance with a government mandate to move all native peoples to a new Indian Territory in Oklahoma. Tom's ancestor was a sixteen-year-old girl at the time, but already recognized by her tribe as a healer. Once in Oklahoma, she never stopped longing to return to her home in Alabama by the river.

A year later, she stole away from the forced encampment in Oklahoma, writing in her journal that "the rivers in Oklahoma do not sing," and, with great courage, began her walk home. It took her five years. Upon hearing her story, Hendrix was moved to spend the next thirty years of his life building a wall of sandstone and limestone to honor her journey. The most moving part of experiencing this mile-long wall, built stone by stone, is its power. Each rock represents one step of her journey, and the height and depth of the wall represent the challenges she faced. It is the largest rock wall built without mortar in the United States. The forced march to Oklahoma was filled with loss and despair for hundreds of native people. But, in creating the wall, Hendrix captured not just the hardship of the walk, but the fire within a seventeen-year-old girl's heart and the power of her loving. Like Viktor Frankl, she did not survive her ordeal angry or bitter. In her surrender to love, the pain was transformed. That love now permeates the stones that honor her.

When the heart fully opens to Spirit, there is an unfolding and a blossoming, just like the opening of a flower as it turns toward the light. We don't surrender to our circumstances; we surrender to love, and love alone. •

Wild Things Tamed

By Ruth Patterson

Bᴀᴄᴋ ɪɴ 1963, Maurice Sendak wrote what has since become a children's classic: *Where the Wild Things Are.* It tells the story of Max, who, having misbehaved, is called a wild thing and is sent to bed without his supper. In his dreams, he goes on a journey to the land of the wild things, who try to terrify him with their roars and threats. He tames them by commanding them to be still and they make him king of all the wild things, leading them in the wild rumpus. But, after a while, Max remembers home. He's lonely. He misses all the good things and, despite their efforts to hold him there, he bids farewell to the wild things and journeys back. He is not the same as he was before his adventure. He arrives back in his very own room to find his supper waiting for him—still hot![1]

For me, transformation implies journey, pilgrimage, a crossing over. It is not something we can will upon ourselves or decide that it should happen to us. Rather, it is something that happens to us as a result, for example, of some experience on the journey or of some encounter. It is gift, and comes either gradually, as we emerge out of the cocoon of a particular way of thinking and being and soar into a new world of awareness, or instantly, as when a new insight impels us across the threshold from a two-dimensional world where everything is cut and dried into a three-dimensional one that is inhabited by wonder, mystery, and an unknowing that is, paradoxically, profoundly recognizable at a level beyond the head.

Odysseus (from whose name we get the word odyssey, meaning a long and epic journey) sets out on his adventures, is lured off-track, and encounters many obstacles before he returns to Ithaca and Penelope as a different person because of his experiences along the way. The wise men in Matthew's Gospel follow the star and succumb fleetingly to the lures of Herod, the wildest "thing" of all. Their epiphany moment occurs in crossing the threshold of the stable at Bethlehem. The wonder and mystery of what has been revealed sends them home by a different route. Life can never be the same. T.S. Eliot gives one of them voice in "Journey of the Magi":

> We returned to our places, these Kingdoms,
> But no longer at ease here, in the old dispensation,
> With an alien people clutching their gods.[2]

THE PRODIGAL SON, finding himself alone among the pigs after the "wild rumpus" in which he squandered his inheritance, is pierced by an awareness of the goodness of his father's house. He sees things differently, from a new vantage point. No longer allowing all things to serve and stroke his smaller self, he begins the journey home, clothed in a newfound humility and a dawning understanding of the mystery of a love that does not wait, but runs to embrace him. With this fresh awareness, he crosses the threshold of home, as if for the first time, and "finds his supper waiting for him" in the form of a huge celebration and affirmation of his sonship.

Zacchaeus, the despised tax collector of Jericho, acting out of character, throws caution to the winds and runs to climb a tree in his passionate desire to see Jesus, the supreme shape-shifter in the story of humankind. The subsequent climbing down, letting go, and unlearning all flow from an encounter that takes place in the hidden intimacy of silence. But the resultant transformation is evident for all to see. Zacchaeus has crossed a threshold into a place of inclusion, generosity, and compassion. No longer do the wild things of avarice, deceit, and cunning roar their terrible roars and show their terrible claws. Half of his possessions he gives to the poor and those whom he

We are propelled forward by an opening heart, by humility, and by a teachable spirit.

has cheated get paid back fourfold. He has come home to his true self.

As I reflect on the odysseys of these and many others, I am struck by the fact that, for each of the protagonists, a crucial part of their journey—that which draws them up short and is a vital element in their transformation—is some form of dis-comfort, dis-ease, or suffering. This is not to say that everyone who experiences hardship or suffering is necessarily transformed into someone who is, in the words of Richard Rohr, a participatory, inclusive, generous self—although it does seem to be either a necessary ingredient or a common denominator for those who are in the process of being transformed (we never reach the end of the process) or, to put it another way, those who are "becoming": coming to be.

Is it an absolute given, an imperative? Perhaps not; perhaps there are a blessed few who find themselves seeing things in a larger and more holistic way without having to enter such shadowy places, but I do not know of any. Threshold crossing implies a letting-go that, in itself, can create struggle, questioning, fear, and grief before we reach a point of recognizing and welcoming the new. We are propelled forward by an opening heart, by humility, and by a teachable spirit. And the irresistible lure that draws us, maybe not immediately identifiable, is an awareness of a deepening, all-pervasive, and inclusive love—one that, in turn, kindles within us a reciprocal love for God (Father, Son, and Holy Spirit), for others, and for self.

The shadowy past of most nations, if not all, is where so many wild things are. The stories about "the other" that have been passed on to us in our tribal groups have been inhabited by monsters—and they are still alive and "well." Outer circumstances may change, but where is transformation? We may think we have become more progressive and enlightened, even more inclusive, forbearing, understanding, and appreciative of diversity. But whenever events in the present are fraught with tension, the monsters manifest themselves again, roaring their terrible roars, gnashing their terrible teeth, rolling their terrible eyes, and showing their terrible claws. Scratch the surface and we find them restlessly waiting only for the command to let the wild rumpus start! Our "once upon a time" becomes, in essence, "all the time." Our best "happily ever after" scenario is a silencing or destruction of the wild thing that is always the other and never, ever us. It does not enter what appears to be, at times, our demonic imagination that there could be another conclusion, one that sees a taming or a disarming that has as much to do with us as it has with the other.

IN THE PRECARIOUS aftermath of the thirty-year conflict in Northern Ireland, much emphasis was placed on the decommissioning of weapons from both "sides." Commissions were set up and trusted people appointed to oversee the process. This required a lot of time, energy, negotiating skills—and money. But what about the attitudes that lay behind the taking up of arms and the holding onto weapons in the first place? Since the 1998 Peace Agreement, we have seen a great many changes, but have we seen transformation? By and large, with a few notable exceptions, I think not.

And why? It is because there has not been an overall decommissioning of minds and hearts. This is always relational, as through presence, encounter, and awareness, people journey to a new place within and, sometimes, without. They cross the threshold to a new way of being. They are no longer at ease in the old dispensation with an alien people still clutching their gods of sectarianism, racism, and fear of the unknown. Their journey has led them away from an "us/them" mentality to an understanding (that is, a standing under) the mystery of a common humanity. Previously clearly demarcated boundaries become gloriously blurred as they begin to recognize, to know again, themselves and everyone else as broken and beloved.

How do I put myself in a place where I can be tipped over into a new way of being? The macro reflects the micro. I cannot expect the world to be transformed if I do not consciously allow myself to be in a place where the likelihood of such a metamorphosis occurring increases. Such a place may be initially uncomfortable, out of character, even alarming. Zacchaeus runs and climbs a tree! The prodigal awakens to the reality of the pig sty. For the wise men, the "stubborn" star does not stop where they imagine it should and so they continue to journey's end—which is also a beginning.

I find a key in Sendak's story. Max tames the wild things by commanding them to be still and then stares at them without blinking. To him, they are no longer frightening. He befriends them. The older I get, the farther I journey, the more I appreciate the challenge, and the invitation, to be still. Initially it can be a fearsome place, where the wild things of multitudinous fears, performance orientation, and regrets strut and roar, posture and threaten to eat me up. But if I remain there in the stillness, I gradually become conscious of the all-pervading presence of the Beloved. As I dare to look at those fears and, on one level, welcome them, I can sense the beginning of a process of decommissioning or taming. Some simply shrivel up and disintegrate, having had no basis in reality. Others, as my understanding of how and why they came to be there grows, lose some of their ferocity and can, almost paradoxically, become gift—what the prophet Isaiah refers to as the treasures of darkness (see 45:3). Through presence, encounter, and awareness, some sort of transformation gives my story fresh elucidation. Gradually, and barely perceptibly, such an epic journey leads me across a threshold where I awaken to the wonder of looking out from a new source. I am being transformed, and such transformation manifests itself in both contemplation and action.

There is much more to such an odyssey, but there is one longing that does not fade, instead increasing in intensity as I attempt to be faithful to putting myself in the place where transformation may continue. It is a "good" ache. It is, in the words of the story, to be where someone loves me best of all. To put it another way, it is the yearning to come home to my true self, to arrive where I started and to recognize it. This is not to be confused with a nostalgic looking-back to a past that, in reality, imprisons, or forward to an ethereal future that anaesthetizes me to the present moment, but rather seeking to live fully in the present with the fiber of my being attuned to inclusion, forbearance, appreciation, and understanding. The call to be homeward-bound in this sense comes to everyone, though not all are aware of it. It is a journey into the broken, yet, paradoxically, whole heart of God. •

Transformation at the Margins

By Mark Longhurst

THE SPIRITUAL PRACTICE of befriending margins is uncomfortable, terrifying, and yet contains transformative power and beauty. The monks producing Ireland's famous ninth-century *Book of Kells*, for example, appreciated the pregnant possibility of margins. They cherished the biblical text itself, of course, but what causes tourists to line up in Trinity College Dublin's Library is something else entirely. People peer into the Library's glass display cases to see the splendid color of ink illuminating letters, Celtic knots tying Gospel text, the oldest Western image of the Virgin Mary, and even hidden cats prowling amidst the first two Greek letters or "Chi Roh" (ΧΡΙΣΤΟΣ) of Christ's name.

To pay attention to margins is to pay attention to how boundary lines are constructed in our world and lives—and then to cross those boundaries. The psyche draws boundaries around what it is willing to face, so exploring unconscious desires through shadow work is a way of welcoming the Holy Spirit to our inner margins. Christian traditions have often neglected, shamed, or marginalized the physical body's wisdom. To begin conscious re-membering of our bodies, then, is essential for integral wholeness. Today, more people are awakening to the way social systems have marginalized society's most vulnerable populations. Prioritizing insights, friendships, and leadership from people on the margins is a way of yielding to holistic political transformation.

For contemplatives to engage margins, especially contemplatives accustomed to the comfortable, majority center, will require the heart's nimble resilience across social space. My own experience befriending Boston's marginal homeless population transformed my sight so I could see homeless people as beautiful bearers of God's image. In 2006, I moved into a scrappy Catholic Worker-inspired community called Haley House. The twelve or so intentional community members operated a soup kitchen from the brownstone building's first floor. On a typical morning, I woke up at 5:25 a.m. and, in a stupor of sleep, rushed to the basement walk-in refrigerator to make breakfast for dozens of men. Fair-trade coffee brewing, I opened the doors for the early arrivals: men who had slept on the street in hidden corners and were eager for grits and a heated room.

One man went by the name "Brother George." He often stumbled in at 7:00 a.m., already drunk. George was a gentle soul. He drew pictures on the day's menu board of a cartoon, tie-wearing man. I didn't know what it meant, but it marked George's signature. He waxed nostalgic about his former days in the Ukraine. "I was a master barber!" he repeated, with flourish, to anyone who would listen. Many of the men invented stories, but I liked to imagine George having his own barbershop, cracking jokes with customers as he gave them a hot shave. Sometimes George laid his head down on the table and wailed

God loves the margins in Jewish and Christian tradition. You could say God colors in them.

in grief. Sometimes he urinated in his pants. When this happened, the other homeless men sat two chairs away from him because the stench was unbearable.

I didn't change George or persuade him to stop drinking. I'm not even sure if he's alive today. But seeing George, day in and day out, changed me: I recognized his intrinsic human beauty and tragedy. I somehow knew that my wholeness was bound up with his wholeness; my wounds connected to his wounds.

In sociological terminology, summarized by biblical scholar Matthew Carter, margins make up a fluid and even ambivalent sphere: Marginal peoples live in the two worlds of both dominant and subordinate spaces of existence. Some wish they could escape margins and taste more of the center. George was a citizen in the world's most powerful and wealthy country, yet he slept on the streets and packed his belongings in a shopping cart.

Alternatively, marginal life is often "over-against." A group at the periphery of a culture or society's center develops subcultures antithetical, even violent or offensive, to those in the center. Marginalized, urban black youth sometimes turn to a marginal drug economy because it seems to be the only employment available. White, working-class Americans sometimes disdain the rhetoric and policies of elite politicians on both left and right. They are "over and against" the center of power.[1]

Jesus is a pioneer of transformation at the margins. Once John the Baptizer dunks Jesus in Jordan's waters, Jesus heads immediately to the wilderness for Satan's testing. The wilderness is that archetypal realm in Hebrew tradition where God initiates and stirs up repentance, which is to say, a revolution of consciousness. It is only after Jesus considers reaching for rocks as bread that he is freed to proclaim: "Repent, for the kingdom of heaven has come near" (see Matthew 4:17). Somehow testing, trials, and margins awaken us to God's nearness.

Margins are nothing less than what Richard Rohr calls "liminal space." From the Latin *limen*, threshold, in liminal space we dwell before, and sometimes dive through, a doorway of transformation. As Fr. Rohr writes in *Adam's Return*,

> Liminality is an inner state and sometimes an outer situation where people can begin to think and act in genuinely new ways.

It is when we are betwixt and between, have left one room but not yet entered the next room, any hiatus between stages of life, jobs, loves, or relationships. It is that graced time when we are not certain or in control, when something genuinely new can happen.[2]

GOD LOVES THE MARGINS in Jewish and Christian tradition. You could say God colors in them. The ancient Israelite story is one of relationship with God through successive marginal identities: first as enslaved brick-workers under the Egyptian empire, then as a liberated but nomadic people. Once landed, ancient Israel nevertheless suffers the marginal fate of a small nation sandwiched between rival imperial powers, vacillating in fealty to Babylonians and Assyrians. They eke out a thriving, if precarious, existence under Kings David and Solomon, only eventually to be crushed and exiled by armies directed by Nebuchadnezzar and Tiglath-Pileser III. The homeless, traumatized yearnings of exile give birth to the tortured cries of Jeremiah's lamentations, but also Isaiah's soaring visions of wholeness: The wolf shall lie down with the lamb, the cow and the bear shall graze.

Christianity's Jewish roots lie in this wilderness-wandering, exiled, and conquered history of ancient Israel. Yet the early Christian movement, first a marginal underground network, famously converted to the center when the Roman Emperor Constantine had a vision of the cross in the sky. He ordered his troops to paint those two Greek Chi-Roh letters of Christ's name on their shields, so that the vertical line of the Rho (P) intersected the center of the Chi (X). Those Celtic monks no doubt had something different in mind.

After millennia of center-dwelling, however, the twenty-first century finds Christianity assuming an increasingly marginal place at the center of culture and power. American Catholic and Mainline Protestant Christians witness ranks shrinking, while growing numbers of people declare "spiritual but not religious" interest. They are affiliated with "None" of the religions or they are "Done" with religion altogether. This exodus carries with it all the panic and grief that accompanies seismic change, but in itself is pregnant with transformative possibility. Western Christianity itself is in a liminal space: Something is dying, and something is being born. The late writer Phyllis Tickle called it a new reformation.

In the synoptic Gospels, Jesus is "transfigured" (which means, in Greek, transformed), not in the Jerusalem Temple, but on a remote mountain in the Galilean countryside (see Matthew 17). Jesus, Peter, James, and John hike up the mountain to pray. They witness a cloud cover the mountain and Jesus' face shine like the sun. Their teacher stands in the tradition of those who dared experience God face-to-face, as one. These are the mystics who risk everything to plunge into the mystery of God's love, glory, and unknowing. Jesus is joined by his Jewish forerunners, Moses and Elijah, each of whom experienced mountaintop transformations themselves, each of whom exemplify the mystical path in that they seek direct, intimate, unmediated relationship with God...at the margins.

Peter, however, symbolizes the center's desire to draw boundaries and distance margins. He humorously offers to build dwellings in which God's glory can rest, but Luke tells us, "Peter did not know what he was talking about" (see Luke 9:33). His suggestion to set up booths, or tents, is a reference to the Jewish Festival of Booths (*Sukkot*). This festival commemorates the Israelites' forty years of wilderness-wandering and tent-dwelling. Tents in Israelite tradition, however, are more than sleeping gear: God—who in those days traveled in the form of a cloud—needed a tent, too, so the Israelites set up what they called a "tent of meeting."

But the Israelites are not content with God dwelling in a tent, and pretty soon a tent becomes a temple. The evolution of God's presence starts in the wilderness margins and, as is all-too-frequent, ends in the Jerusalem center. David and Solomon eventually oversee a massive building project to house God's glory. Peter, bless his heart, wishes to do the same.

There's nothing wrong with temples, but the problem arises when the center is prioritized at the expense of the margins. Years later, Christian monarchs build basilicas, sanctuaries, and altars to house God. These religious centers are beautiful, but become sites where God resides, all too often, to the exclusion of marginal people and places. The religious, Jerusalem-dwelling leaders in Jesus' day said: "Nothing good can come from Nazareth" (see John 1:46). Followers of Jesus, then and now, think differently—such as today's evangelical new monastics that move into the "abandoned places of Empire."[3]

The threshold of margins is accompanied by fire, and fire is the painful part of transformation. The Celtic poet and author John

O'Donohue points out that the word "threshold" is etymologically related to threshing, which is what farmers do when they separate grain from chaff. John the Baptizer predicted this would be indicative of Jesus' way when he envisioned Jesus holding a winnowing fork in his hand at the threshing floor (see Matthew 3:12). Christians turned the image into hell's torment and thus missed the metaphor: Entering a liminal threshold involves threshing, or a necessary stripping down. As O'Donohue says, "threshold is a place where you move into more critical and challenging and worthy fullness."[4]

The present moment may be asking us, now and always, to embrace the power and wisdom of the margins—or, as writer-activist Teresa Pasquale Mateus says, to "center the margins." For white people coming from privileged backgrounds, this may mean non-defensive, open-hearted listening to the marginalized life experiences of black and brown Americans. Once hearts are cracked open, for example, to hear the horror of African American experiences, first of slavery and lynching, and now of incarceration, the war on drugs, and gun violence, it becomes a transformative human response to affirm with weeping, prayer, solidarity, and action that black lives matter. Once hearts are cracked open to hear and honor immigrant and refugee stories, our hearts become broken at America's long legacy of turning away or disenfranchising those who differ from the white mold. And, once hearts are broken, it ceases to become an ideology for people of privilege to stand with the marginalized. Solidarity with the different is transformed into simply a natural human response of compassion, reflecting our inherent, yet fragmented, oneness.

If margins are where God colors and spends time, then margins are holy sites beckoning us toward greater wholeness. They query what we think we know and invite us to a listening posture toward life. To some, this might feel like an annihilation of our identity, because the answers margins hold destabilize the center's certainties. This is full of possibility, but never easy, and often excruciating. The threshold of transformation is, indeed, a narrow gate.   •

Coming to Our Senses:

Wisdom Interventions for a Troubled World

By Brittian Bullock and Mike Morrell

READING FROM THE SACRED BOOKS

I N OUR ESSAY, "Evolving Wild: Glimpses of the Garden City," in
the "Evolutionary Thinking" issue of *Oneing*, we pull two "books"
from the Library of Wisdom, dusting them off for civilized humanity's consideration: the revered Book of Scripture, and the equally
sacred Book of Nature, as exegeted by anthropologists, archeologists,
and ecologists.

We acknowledge that Axial Age religion, as revealed through the
Abrahamic faiths, emerged in the past three thousand years. Juda-
ism, Christianity, and Islam safeguard an oral tradition describing

the human journey over the past twelve thousand years—a pivotal transition from hunting and gathering to settled agriculture. That three thousand years is an eye-blink of geologic time for a four-million-year-old species. We believe the Book of Nature has much to teach us about these "silent" years in our four-million-year saga.

We also believe the Book of Scripture has more to say about this primordial state of Original Blessing—and our subsequent transition to greater complexity and isolation—than we ordinarily notice.

Original, indigenous, global human culture—before the advent of farming and cities as we know them today—was high-touch, high-contact, egalitarian, and presence-oriented. This created what renowned attachment psychologist Mary Ainsworth called an "environment of evolutionary adaptivity,"[1] a fluid-yet-grounded human culture marked by secure attachment and emotional regulation.

As we outlined in "Evolving Wild," the transition from immediate-return foraging to complex agriculture signaled an even more profound shift in the inner lives of our species: Instead of human culture continuing to be as innate to people as dolphin culture is to dolphins, suddenly—from the vantage point of geologic time—humanity became a self-obscuring enigma.

Once a primal unity, incorporating our sense of the sacred, ourselves, each other, and our environment, humanity experienced a kind of *reverse baptism*, the waters of our belovedness being wrung from our pores.

In an epochal moment, we found ourselves alone, naked, and cast out of the garden. We've been trying to get back ever since.

Religion—from the Latin *religare*, "to bind (back) together"—is about attempting to reunite what has been scattered. And yet, if we're honest, religion has a mixed track record at best. For every hospital maintained, sublime art created, or devotion cultivated at the apex of religion's best, there's a war justified, persecution begun, or joy-draining stinginess perpetuated at the nadir of religion's worst.

The challenge we're facing is that *it's difficult to transcend our omni-directional loneliness from the same level of being that created it.* Axial Age, Fertile Crescent religion was born out of the anguish of alienation. It can't be expected to pull the full freight of four-fold reunion with God, self, others, and planet—Divine revelation or no. For "we see through a glass darkly" (St. Paul; see 1 Corinthians 13:12), but "we get by with a little help from our friends" (Sts. Paul, John, George, and Ringo).[2] The "cures" propagated by civilization's religion and spirituality are worth noting, but they contain at least a drop of its self-same poison. The antidote can be found in our *friends*, namely the human and more-than-human world that existed ages prior to our iteration, *homo civilizationus*. In the apocalyptic ruminations of Revelation, we read that God in Christ is the one who "was and is and is yet to come" (see Revelation 1:8). Drawing on this resonant past, present, and future visioneering, we've identified dozens of *ancestral wisdom interventions*, spanning from our inner lives to the macro-organizing of our planet. Here we're going to examine a powerful pair:

- Contemplation
- Communion-in-Community

We call these "interventions" because they interrupt our mechanical thinking, our normal "octaves of being," with a *different* melody that invites genuine conscious response and a shift to a stable state of unitive seeing. But we're often inoculated against the power of these interventions by a weakened strain of each. In order to recover the potency of each intervention, a little excavation is in order.

CONTEMPLATION

LET'S FACE IT: Mindfulness is all the rage these days. From your corner yoga studio to corporate meditative boot camps to—we have to say it—increasingly commodified Christian culture, boutique forms of altered states of consciousness are served up to us in bite-sized, pay-to-play servings. But what in the world does mindfulness, or what the Christian tradition calls contemplation, really teach?[3]

Contemplation is, in essence, the experience of waking up, moment after moment, to the here-and-now. To *contemplate* literally means "to observe"; it's the function of seeing with increasing clarity. It is a seamless field of vision where we see ourselves, not only as separate beings, but also as an intractable part of a greater whole. This may very well be described in mystical terms, but it's important to note that this is the reality of consciousness in any lens.

Clear-eyed and unconditional acceptance of what-is seems to have been written into the core of Jesus' being.

Indeed, the tendency to refer to contemplation in primarily supernatural language clues us in to how truly foreign *actually observing reality* is. This is why much of even the Christian contemplative stream describes the peak of contemplative attainment as an *altered state* rather than a *stable stage* of awareness; the goal becomes an ecstatic "union" with an external deity rather than unitive seeing of all that is. Cynthia Bourgeault summarizes the difference between these approaches succinctly:

> Mysticism means seeing Oneness.
> Unitive Seeing means seeing *from* Oneness.

Anthropologists often comment about a perceptibly different way of seeing among hunter-gatherer cultures. The tribesperson stands still, eyes neither fixed nor searching. There is an expansive gaze with which hunters consider their environment. It feels alert, but grounded. Without romanticizing what is potentially an essential survival mechanism, we witness a kind of heightened awareness—a connection to the spontaneous pantheon of the present moment. Strict joy sweeps the construct of time out of the mind, gifting us with the *phenomenology of experience*.

Cultural commentator Morris Berman, in *Wandering God*, asks:

> Shall we call this experience "sacred"? The problem with this is that it is a modern (i.e. civilized) way of relating to it. For Hunter-Gatherer societies, there was not a separate category of existence called "the sacred." When Native Americans refer to the Great Spirit, they often are talking about the wind. This spirit is "merely" creation itself.[4]

This experience is, in short, what we might refer to as "living in the moment" or simply being conscious. It is pure immanence, bringing with it a felt sense of what civilized religion often considers transcendence.

Is it any wonder that almost every spiritual and wisdom tradition since that time has included some attempt at recovering our roots of living in the present?

Jesus seems to be keenly aware of unitive consciousness and the practice of *observation* or contemplation. We see him frequently slowing down the fast pace of life—even his ostensibly important "work" of preaching, healing, and travelling—by withdrawing to quiet places to pray alone or with a few of his disciples (see Luke 6:12, 9:18, 22:39). It's his attention to *what is*—whether the lilies of the field or the conditions of people's hearts—that most demonstrates an exquisite contemplative awareness.

Watchfulness. Awareness. Observation. Clear-eyed and unconditional acceptance of what-is seems to have been written into the core of Jesus' being. Jesus is not providing a novel way of living, per se, but is instead reminding us what it means to be quintessentially human. He is calling us to rediscover our biological baseline.

COMMUNION-IN-COMMUNITY

I F UNITIVE SIGHT or contemplation is a foundational ancestral wisdom intervention, then the house built on this foundation is a feasting-house. The practice of *conviviality*—or relationship-nourishing meal-sharing—is a lost art.

For many, eating today is almost a necessary evil, something accomplished through "fast" food on one end of the spectrum and accompanied with much hand-wringing over ever-changing health and foodie purity codes on the other end. Somewhere between Big Macs and arugula, we've lost the plot.

By following the foraging trails of our earliest ancestors, we can see that eating was a way to hearts as well as stomachs. The meal, when practiced with contemplative awareness, is actually a statement of values. Let's set this table for you.

Foraging societies, such as early hunter-gatherers, are considered *immediate-return* cultures. This means that, if they're hungry, they eat. They partake of what's there. They consume it—all. Immediate-return cultures don't store up surplus, hoard, or plan for their retirement in the distant future.[5] Interestingly, a distinct effect of this routine is that resources are shared. Most archeologists concur that these ancient peoples were egalitarian in their distribution of resources. Women, men, and children participated equally in what was available.

After tens of thousands of years, this mutuality ended as the complexity of tribal culture increased. *Sedentism*, and with it agricultural and pastoral technique, required the cultivating and stockpiling of surplus and strategizing for future endeavors. Scientists call these newer societies (ours among them) *delayed-return* cultures, precisely because gratification is delayed until the next season or the next harvest.

During this difficult transition, the importance of feasting came into view. The *feast* in early agricultural societies was a way of memorializing the older human experience of sharing across gender, power, and all other lines. Ancient feasts would have contained a kind of magical remembrance of earlier egalitarianism.

It is impossible to note any of this and not immediately be drawn to Passover in Hebrew Scripture[6]: a meal, on the run, shared by households, in which everything was consumed. This commemorative feast tells an important story, not only of life and God's provision, but also of immediacy and familial connection.

Within the New Testament, the feast of Passover took on an even greater significance as it became what Christians refer to as the Eucharist. In the early church it was a literal meal, not only a sip of wine and a wafer. Jesus himself imbued the meal with fresh force. By savoring this ancient feast, his followers were both partaking of and becoming the mystical body of Christ. This became, in a manner of speaking, Jesus' signature move.[7] However, it was the church-planter Paul of Tarsus who seems to have really seized the revolutionary import of Eucharist in nourishing community.

In his letter to the Corinthians, Paul is addressing apparent divisions within the friends and followers of Jesus. They're at each other's throats, due to breaches in trust. Apparently idolatry, incest, drunkenness, and sleeping with temple prostitutes were all going on within the young community. But most appalling to Paul was the *relational* behavior that took place during the Eucharistic meal. For him, this meal had the power to transform, and the church's failure to see this put everything in jeopardy. This meal symbolizes inherent wholeness within the family of faith. Just as we break the bread, he argues, we partake of one loaf (see 1 Corinthians 10:16–17). He rebukes the Corinthians for their selfish and inconsiderate conduct during their gatherings (1 Corinthians 11:20–22a):

> When you come together, it is not the Lord's Supper you eat, for as you eat, each of you goes ahead without waiting for anybody else. One remains hungry, another gets drunk. Don't you have homes to eat and drink in? Or do you despise the church of God and humiliate those who have nothing?

Communion re-institutes the ancient rhythm of eating together as egalitarian practice. It is the physical remembrance that we are not separate from one another. The meal itself becomes the ritualized practice of unitive consciousness.

What Paul, and Jesus before him were emphasizing is a dramatic new sort of social engineering, which attempts to build a new culture from the ground up on the principles of egalitarianism. This Divine Supper Club affirmed each member, regardless of social distinction, as having unique importance and being worthy of full participation. This simple, subversive act challenged the dominant order of patriarchy, hierarchy, and the established norms of civilization. So where does all this bring us? What does it matter if we observe the world clear-eyed, through contemplative seeing? How will it change us if we routinely share resplendently across all social divisions? Simply this: These interventions shift our core beingness. By rooting ourselves in the grace of right now, and participating in open-handed, open-hearted community, we can begin to experience and embody the wholeness of connection that is our birthright as a species, taking our rightful place in the circle of life. It is here that real healing can begin. •

NOTES

Transformation

1 James P. Danaher, *Jesus after Modernity: A 21st-Century Critique of Our Modern Concept of Truth and the Truth of the Gospel* (Eugene, OR: Pickwick, 2011).

2 See Matthew 7:12. This also appears in all of the major world religions.

The Heart of Deep Change

1 Richard Rohr, *The Naked Now: Learning to See as the Mystics See* (New York: Crossroad Publishing, 2009), 53.

2 David G. Benner, *Human Being and Becoming: Living the Adventure of Life and Love* (Grand Rapids, MI: Brazos Press, 2016). Chapter 5 presents a much fuller discussion of egoic consciousness while chapter 6 examines how it compares to heart-based consciousness.

3 For a more detailed mapping of the transformational journey and extensive discussion of its essential dynamics, see David G. Benner, *Spirituality and the Awakening Self: The Sacred Journey of Transformation* (Grand Rapids, MI: Brazos Press, 2012).

4 See Juliet Benner, *Contemplative Vision: A Guide to Christian Art and Prayer* (Downer's Grove, IL: InterVarsity Press, 2010) for more on the use of art as a heart-based tool for awakening.

The Bell Rack of My Selfhood

1 T. S. Eliot, "Four Quartets," http://www.davidgorman.com/4Quartets/.

2 As quoted in Cynthia Bourgeault, *The Holy Trinity and the Law of Three: Discovering the Radical Truth at the Heart of Christianity* (Boston: Shambhala, 2013), 117.

3 Helen M. Luke, *Old Age* (New York: Parabola, 1987), 95.

4 Leonard Cohen, "Anthem," http://www.azlyrics.com/lyrics/leonardcohen/anthem.html.

Four Shapes to Transformation

1 William Wordsworth, "French Revolution," *The Complete Poetical Works* (London: Macmillan, 1888; Bartleby.com, 1999), http://www.bartleby.com/145/ww285.html.

Divine Patience

1 Rainer Maria Rilke, *Letters to a Young Poet*, trans. Charlie Louth (New York: Penguin, 2011), 10.

2 Ibid., 19.

3 Ibid., 24.

4 C. Otto Scharmer, *Theory U* (San Francisco: Berrett-Koehler, 2009), 41.

The Well

1 "The Well," *Pilgrim: Poems by David Whyte* (Langley, WA: Many Rivers Press, 2012), 18. Used with permission.

Repairing My Inner Two States

1 Julian of Norwich, *Revelations of Divine Love*, chapter 61.

A Surrender to Love

1 Rainer Maria Rilke, "You, Darkness," http://www.poetry.net/poem/29754.

2 Robert Browning, "From 'Paraclesus,'" http://www.bartleby.com/236/102.html.

Wild Things Tamed

1 Maurice Sendak, *Where the Wild Things Are* (Harmondsworth, Middlesex, UK: Penguin Books, 1970).

2 T.S. Eliot, "Journey of the Magi," *The Waste Land and Other Poems* (London: Faber and Faber, 1972), 66.

Transformation at the Margins

1 Sociological definitions of margins are from Warren Carter, *Matthew and the Margins: A Sociopolitical and Religious Reading* (Maryknoll, NY: Orbis, 2000), 45.

2 Richard Rohr, *Adam's Return: The Five Promises of Male Initiation* (New York: Crossroad, 2004), 135.

3 Rutba House, *School(s) for Conversion: 12 Marks of a New Monasticism* (Eugene, OR: Cascade Books, 2005), xii.

4 Quoted in Krista Tippett, *Becoming Wise: An Inquiry into the Mystery and Art of Living* (New York: Penguin, 2016), 76.

Coming to Our Senses:
Wisdom Interventions for a Troubled World

1 Darcia Narvaez et al., eds., *Evolution, Early Experience and Human Development: From Research to Practice and Policy* (New York: Oxford University Press, 2012), 31.

2 See The Beatles, "With a Little Help from My Friends," *Sgt. Pepper's Lonely Hearts Club Band*, 1967.

3 For trenchant critiques of the consumerist co-opting of mindfulness and embodiment practices in Buddhism and yoga, respectively, see https://theconversation.com/how-corporates-co-opted-the-art-of-mindfulness-to-make-us-bear-the-unbearable-47768, http://salon.com/2015/09/27/corporate_mindfulness_is_bullsht_zen_or_no_zen_youre_working_harder_and_being_paid_less, and http://decolonizingyoga.com. From a Christian perspective, see William T. Cavanaugh, *Being Consumed: Economics and Christian Desire* (Grand Rapids: Eerdmans, 2008).

4 Morris Berman, *Wandering God: A Study in Nomadic Spirituality* (New York: State University of New York Press, 2000), 11.

5 Compare this ancestral trait to the fascinating instructions that Moses and Aaron relay about how to handle the miraculous manna in Exodus 16!

6 See Exodus 12–13, Deuteronomy 16.

7 See Matthew 26:17–30, Mark 14:12–26, Luke 22:7–39, and John 13:1–17:26.

Center for
Action and
Contemplation

A collision of opposites forms the cross of Christ.
One leads downward preferring the truth of the humble.
The other moves leftward against the grain.
But all are wrapped safely inside a hidden harmony:
One world, God's cosmos, a benevolent universe.